MOTIVATION-BASED INTERVIEWING

MOTIVATION-BASED INTERVIEWING

A Revolutionary Approach to Hiring the Best

Foreword by Lee Cockerell, author of *Creating Magic: 10 Common Sense Leadership Strategies from a Life at Disney*

Carol Quinn

Society for Human Resource Management
Alexandria, Virginia
www.shrm.org

Strategic Human Resource Management India
Mumbai, India
www.shrmindia.org

Society for Human Resource Management
Haidian District Beijing, China
www.shrm.org/cn

Society for Human Resource Management, Middle East and Africa Office
Dubai, UAE
www.shrm.org/pages/mena.aspx

SOCIETY FOR HUMAN
RESOURCE MANAGEMENT

This publication is designed to provide accurate and authoritative information regarding the subject matter covered. It is sold with the understanding that neither the publisher nor the author is engaged in rendering legal or other professional service. If legal advice or other expert assistance is required, the services of a competent, licensed professional should be sought. The federal and state laws discussed in this book are subject to frequent revision and interpretation by amendments or judicial revisions that may significantly affect employer or employee rights and obligations. Readers are encouraged to seek legal counsel regarding specific policies and practices in their organizations.

Disclaimer: No promise, expressed or implied, of any specific results is made by the publisher or the author with regard to the use of motivation-based interviewing. The quality of employee selection and hiring is dependent upon numerous factors including but not limited to how well MBI is implemented, the quality of interview questions, and the interviewer's skill level, knowledge, openness to learn, attitude, and objectivity. Interviewers are solely responsible for their own hiring results.

This book is published by the Society for Human Resource Management (SHRM). The interpretations, conclusions, and recommendations in this book are those of the author and do not necessarily represent those of the publisher.

MBI, the interviewing methodology, is the intellectual property of Hire Authority, Inc.

This publication may not be reproduced, stored in a retrieval system, or transmitted in whole or in part, in any form or by any means, electronic, mechanical, photocopying, recording, or otherwise, without the prior written permission of the publisher, or authorization through payment of the appropriate per-copy fee to the Copyright Clearance Center, Inc., 222 Rosewood Drive, Danvers, MA 01923, 978-750-8600, fax 978-646-8600, or on the Web at www.copyright.com. Requests to the publisher for permission should be addressed to SHRM Book Permissions, 1800 Duke Street, Alexandria, VA 22314, or online at http://www.shrm.org/about-shrm/pages/copyright--permissions.aspx. SHRM books and products are available on most online bookstores and through the SHRMStore at www.shrmstore.org.

The Society for Human Resource Management is the world's largest HR professional society, representing 285,000 members in more than 165 countries. For nearly seven decades, the Society has been the leading provider of resources serving the needs of HR professionals and advancing the practice of human resource management. SHRM has more than 575 affiliated chapter within the United States and subsidiary offices in China, India, and United Arab Emirates. Please visit

Library of Congress Cataloging-in-Publication Data has been applied for and is on file with the Library of Congress.

ISBN (pbk): 978-1-586-44547-8; ISBN (PDF): 978-1-586-44548-5;
ISBN (EPUB): 978-1-586-44549-2; ISBN (Mobi): 978-1-586-44550-8

Printed in the United States of America

FIRST EDITION

PB Printing   10 9 8 7 6 5 4 3 2 1   61.14518

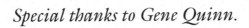

Special thanks to Gene Quinn.

Table of Contents

Foreword

Carol Quinn is the creator of motivation-based interviewing (MBI). She has a lifetime of interviewing experience and is the expert of experts on hiring. I thought I was great at selecting the right people in my long career at Hilton Hotels, Marriott International, and The Walt Disney Company until I learned about the methods in MBI. There is nothing more important than the people you bring into your organization. Nothing! If you have been to Disney you know we have the best Cast Members in the world and that is not by accident. We look for passion, attitude, and skill. Skill is trainable, while passion and attitude are not.

As someone who currently works with organizations all around the world, I have found that most people with interviewing and hiring responsibility have had no formal training on a consistent, effective method for making their hiring decisions. The other problem is the Internet. Most applicants have learned to go online and learn all of the answers to the typical behavior-based interview questions that you're likely to ask. There are no questions allowing for a yes-or-no answer in MBI. It does not allow applicants to deliver soft answers to any of the interviewer's questions. Instead, it challenges applicants to share specific details and explain how they dealt with the obstacles they have encountered in past positions. Interviewers who have learned MBI know how to recognize when an applicant is trying to mask the lack of details with a good-sounding answer. Interviewers won't be fooled by these responses anymore. MBI is about asking effective interview questions and using effective interviewing techniques to get the applicant information needed to make great hiring decisions.

When it comes to an organization's success, the most important thing is hiring. If you don't get hiring right, nothing else matters.

Carol's first book on MBI titled *Don't Hire Anyone Without Me!* was excellent, but her updated version (with a new title) is the best book ever written on the topic of interviewing and hiring. This newly titled second edition, *Motivation-Based Interviewing: Anniversary Edition*, is a must-read! I guarantee you that after studying and putting into practice Carol's MBI method you will experience a dramatic increased success rate in your selection of team members, and that is a win for you, your customers, your team, and the bottom line.

Make sure you train everyone in your organization who has any responsibility for interviewing and hiring. You will be glad you did. The formula for excellence in any organization is to hire them right, train them right and treat them right!

—Lee Cockerell, former executive vice president of Disney World and the author of four best-selling books, including *The Customer Rules, Creating Magic, Time Management Magic,* and *Career Magic.*

Introduction

For most people in the corporate world, hiring is just one responsibility of many. For me, it's different. Hiring is my passion, without a doubt. I knew it in college when I had that monotone professor for Personnel Management 101. You know the type; all we saw was the back of his head because the entire class time consisted of him writing on the whiteboard. To make matters worse, the textbook was dry and it had no pictures. All the students complained to each other that this class was a "snoozefest." But yours truly aced that class. I found the material absolutely fascinating.

From there I went to work for an employment agency. A year later, I opened my own agency. Over the years, I attended every workshop and seminar I could to learn more about hiring. I became familiar with behavior-based interviewing, competency-based selection, targeted selection, and other techniques. The workshops and seminars all promised that if I followed the prescribed process, I would hire great employees. But you know what? Sometimes I did and sometimes I didn't. Those bad hires still seemed to slip through—too much for my liking. Something was still lacking in the process. After all, if you could hire someone great one time, why couldn't you repeat this result more often?

After spending many years in Corporate America in the hiring arena, a nationwide retail organization employed me to revamp their management selection process. In their early years, a secretary was promoted to become their first recruiter. She developed the process that was in place when I arrived. Facing a double-digit growth phase, the organization recognized the need to improve both how they hired and whom they hired. For a period of three months, while their old process was being dismantled and replaced with a new process I created, I handled the entire interview process myself;

I was the only interviewer and the sole decision-maker of which management candidate got hired and which didn't.

This had the potential to turn out very good for me, or very bad. Think about it—it would be one thing if these candidates were being hired to work for me, but I was the gateway for everyone's future employees. The first time their bosses would meet them was when they showed up for work. If my hires were better than before, there would be a lot of praise to reap. On the other hand, if the supervisors were not satisfied with their new hires' performance, I (justifiably) would receive the blame.

You can tell by the fact that I am writing this book that it turned out for the better—the hires were better, turnover dropped, and the cost-per-hire decreased. One of the best benefits for me personally was the important learning opportunity of tracking these hires' ongoing performance: I could compare a candidate's pre-hire interview with their post-hire performance for a year or longer. I could also compare their job performance to those hired before I came onboard.

Guess what? Those who interviewed the best and even those who had the most skills and work experience were not always the ones who performed in the top 20 percent. And within the group of top performers, there were those who were not the most skilled or the most experienced at the time of their hire. Some of the better job performers hadn't even interviewed well but were hired anyway. What *exactly* was it that the high achievers had in common that was missing in others, even in those possessing great skills, and—most importantly—how could it be distinguished during the interviewing process?

The pursuit of this missing piece or pieces taunted me for quite a while. I couldn't settle for hit-and-miss hiring results. I wanted to know how to hire well *and* how to do it consistently. I kept these questions in the back of my mind as I conducted hundreds of interviews, day in and day out. Gradually the answers started to reveal themselves. Long story short, I came to realize that how interviewers had been going about assessing a candidate's motivation was all wrong! As it turns out, candidates who possess the best skills to do the job may or may not be the best people to hire. To hire well, interviewers must have a greater understanding of motivation to be able to correctly distinguish those who are genuinely self-motivated from those who will need to be motivated to do their job. Some skilled candidates lack the right kind of attitude, while others are missing the passion for doing the work—two key components that fuels the high achiever's self-motivation. Knowing what I know today, I'd put my money on the candidate with the most self-motivation to do the job, hands down! Motivation-based interviewing fills in the missing pieces when it comes to hiring, and it's already revolutionizing how we hire. This second-edition MBI book (formerly titled *Don't Hire Anyone Without Me!*) will change how we hire forever.

Chapter 1
The State of Hiring

In the past, I've had my share of hiring success stories, just like most interviewers have. I've also hired plenty of people who fell into that average-performer category. But oh, the pain of a bad hire! I don't know which I focused on more—hiring high performers or simply avoiding bad hires. Clearly some bad hires are worse than others, but none are a pleasant experience. I recall one particular hire in my early years of interviewing. His first day on the job was supposed to include getting on an airplane and flying to the corporate office to begin management training. As it turned out, he figured out a way to cash in the airline ticket we gave him and neither he nor the money was ever seen or heard from again. Then there was the time I was ready to expand my recruiting agency. It was a one-person operation with yours truly doing all the work, which became too much to handle. It was time for me to hire my first employee. I was very careful in my selection process, and quite confident in my abilities. After all, I was a successful recruiter and had already interviewed hundreds of job candidates! The person I selected came with interviewing and hiring experience as well as management experience. She seemed like a hard worker and expressed a profound interest in the job. On top of that, I liked her. However, much to my dismay, it turned out to be a total disaster! For the next few months, she had one excuse after another for not meeting her goals and her lack of productivity. Initially I felt compassion towards her hard-luck stories and gave her the benefit of doubt. Since she wasn't bringing in much revenue, the cost to retain her was putting a financial strain on the business. That hiring choice caused me so much stress! I would have been better off if I had never hired her and did all the work myself. I almost lost the business because of one poor hiring decision. The good part, however, is that experience got the wheels turning in my head: *how did I get it so wrong?*

After thousands of interviews, along with tracking the job performance of those hired, I discovered the real difference between high performers and everyone else. It's not how eager a person is to *get* the job, or even about their bounty of skills, but rather, it's how eager a person is to *do* the job. The million-dollar question was, how could I make this distinction *before* they were hired? I knew the answer would lead me to a place where I could genuinely tell the difference between the great hires and the not-so-great ones. Then it hit me: *everything revolves around how we assess self-motivation.*

Speaking of Motivation...

Motivating employees has always been a hot topic in the business world. As supervisors, we're continuously trying to come up with ways to prod workers to take action, produce results, and achieve higher goals. We spend countless hours seeking ways to make workers want to perform better. We coach and counsel. We dangle carrots. Sometimes we discipline and threaten job loss just to get them to do the job they were hired to do. Around the turn of the century, this age-old problem got a new name: "unmotivated employees" are now called "disengaged employees" and the act of motivating employees became "employee engagement." It's the same problem—unmotivated employees—just a new name.

Have you ever noticed that the word "motivation" is often preceded by the word "self"? One would think we could just say a person is motivated or isn't. But somewhere along the line, someone attached the word "self" to the word "motivation" to make a distinction. When we refer to motivation, we aren't automatically talking about the ability to put one*self* into motion, not at all. This is where many interviewers go astray. They think all they have to do is assess whether or not a candidate is motivated.

So, go ahead and ask a candidate about his motivation. Ask him, on a scale of one to ten, how much effort he puts into his work or how important he thinks initiative is. Or how about a candidate who finished a project. Can we assume she is motivated? The project got done and that's what counts, right? What if the boss told her prior to the project, "If you miss this project deadline the way you have missed so many others, you'll be fired"? What if the boss constantly had to check up on her progress and push her when she lagged behind? What if this employee made excuses and argued with her boss, insisting that the boss was being unreasonable, that there was no way it could all get done? What if the employee spent too much time on the phone or took long smoke breaks? The project may have gotten finished barely on time. But during a job interview, this person can brag about how she finished a tough project. Only talking about the success of the project and conveniently leaving out the details about the boss's push, this candidate probably appears to have been self-motivated. But she wasn't. She had trouble with the "self" part.

If you fail to assess motivation correctly during the interviewing process, you can become the proud supervisor of employees who lack self-motivation and will be dependent on *you* to motivate them—also known as employee engagement. Too often these people slip through the screening process and are hired.

How Are We Really Doing at Hiring?

Organizations spend a tremendous amount of time, money, and resources teaching managers how to motivate employees as a way to improve the organization's overall performance and success, yet put forth very little effort training interviewers.

I think a little healthy introspection might offer some enlightenment. Ask yourself these questions: Why do we assume we have hired well when the employee is underperforming? Did they change or did we miss the mark? If the act of motivating employees is so effective, why then do we still have unmotivated or disengaged employees? Why do we think trying to fundamentally change another human being is a better strategy than fixing the selection process?

So then, what is the state of hiring and why is it important that we know the answer to this question? It's important because many interviewers and many organizations believe they are already doing a fine job at selecting their employees. This belief comes with a side effect: not being open to learning and implementing a better way. After all, what is there to improve when you're already good at hiring? Before we can leap into motivation-based interviewing, we must start by opening our minds. Knowing where the employee selection process is going awry is how we open our minds. There is a good chance that what you have always known to be true about interviewing and hiring, whether that's a little or a lot, is about to get disrupted. It's important to understand where we are today and why much of what we are doing when it comes to hiring is broken. I recommend that you sit down and buckle your seatbelt. You're in for a ride!

Untrained Interviewers

This is a good place to start. Over the past two decades, in the Hire Authority interviewer training workshops, attendees have been asked to raise their hand if they've never received any kind of formal training on how to interview. More than 80 percent raise their hands. Let's think about this; we have a lot of hiring managers out there who have never been properly trained on conducting interviews and making hiring decisions. What are we thinking? Do we believe there are no negative ramifications for hiring mistakes? Do we believe we have the power to change bad hires into high performers?

Imagine yourself for a moment sitting in the pilot seat of a commercial airplane that's in flight. You've never flown a plane or had any training and now you're told that you're the new pilot. There's a fairly good chance you're going to crash! This scenario is totally absurd, of course, but it is similar to promoting people into management and giving them the responsibility of interviewing and making hiring decisions without ever teaching them how. Many managers are essentially winging it when it comes to selecting new employees. Several years ago, after an onsite motivation-based interviewing workshop, a director-level executive came up to thank me. He said he had been interviewing for nineteen years and admitted he'd never really felt confident that he knew what he was doing when it came to hiring. He said he wasn't terrible at it, but he'd had his share of hiring mistakes. He finally felt that he received the training that would help him hire better. He said that he wished he'd had the opportunity to learn this information nineteen years sooner.

Of the 20 percent or fewer who had received training, most say it was some interviewing basics, legal dos and don'ts, and behavior-based interviewing, none of which will help any interviewer correctly or consistently hire high performers. When you think about this, there is no way anyone can believe we're getting the best possible hiring results under these circumstances. But it doesn't stop here. It gets worse.

Behavior-Based Interviewing

Next let's tackle behavior-based interviewing. There is so much wrong with it that using it is likely to erode your quality-of-hire.

Decades ago, when behavior-based interviewing was first introduced, I—like many of us—thought it was great. Considering where we had come from (e.g., gut instinct, the introduction of open-ended and hypothetical questions), behavior-based interviewing seemed great. However, after using it for a while we have come to discover it produces extreme hit-and-miss hiring results, and there are a lot of reasons why. Behavior-based interviewing is like interviewing in the Wild West: there are few rules, no minimum hiring standard, and almost anything goes. There's an infinite amount of bad behavior-based interview questions, along with instructions on how to answer them well, posted all over the Internet. Many of the questions are so ineffective they actually help candidates provide overly positive answers, causing interviewers to give unjustified high ratings. This wouldn't be a problem if each candidate actually performed at that level, but that's not the case. We have a big problem with underperforming employees because of this overrating. Ineffective interview questions gather candidate information that is unsuitable for use in predicting future performance, yet that's exactly what is being used to make hiring decisions. This is why behavior-based interviewing is essentially unreliable for identifying high performers.

Job Skills

One of the most common misconceptions in hiring is that skill level equates to job performance level—*the better the skills, the better the job performance.* Skill simply means the person can do the job, not that they will actually do it.

Hiring based on skill level alone is not the answer. Think about it: if it were all about skill, we would not need to interview anyone. We could hire everyone and teach them the necessary job skills, and 100 percent would be high performers. We would never have to terminate anyone either; we would simply fill their skill gaps so they too would become high performers. But we know it doesn't work this way, and that's because it takes more than just skill to succeed.

Skills are useless without the initiative to apply them. The world is filled with people who lack the initiative or motivation to do what it takes to make full use of their potential. Some skilled employees may lack motivation, while some unskilled or underskilled employees may be highly driven to achieve. Therefore, hiring well is more than measuring skills. If one relies on skills alone as the determining factor for hiring, the results can be employee job performance that ranges from very good to very bad, which is why most organizations employ the full gamut of performers. Hiring results become more about luck rather than effective interviewing. Skills and motivation go hand in hand, but they are assessed in very different ways.

Because of its limitations, it is impossible to correctly assess motivation using behavior-based interviewing. However, motivation-based interviewing aligns with what brings achievement and success about, making it far more effective at accurately identifying high performers.

Predicting Future Behavior

Behavior-based interviewing works on the principle that past behavior is the best predictor of future behavior. The problem with this is that it infers that a candidate's past behavior will repeat exactly the same way in the future. It suggests that they behave in only one way and are therefore predictable, but behaviors can and do vary. People may be on their best behavior or their worst behavior, but that doesn't mean they are *always* that good or *always* that bad. What is important to interviewers is how a person behaves *most* of the time. This is a much better predictor of future performance. Examples of infrequent behavior only provide insight to how a person will behave occasionally, leaving their normal, everyday behavior unknown.

Here's an analogy that may help: Imagine every example of past behavior that a candidate shares with you during the interview as either a green ball or a blue ball. In this example, the green balls are symbolic of the candidate's infrequent behavior. The blue ones represent the candidate's most consistent behavior. The blue ones are most important because they signify behavior that it is likely to continue occurring on a regular basis, also known as a person's predominant behavior.

If we want to predict how the candidate will perform from day to day as a norm, we must not be colorblind to these blue and green balls. Interviewers go astray because they can't see a difference, or they don't know that a difference exists. They assume all examples of behavior will exactly mirror future performance. Without knowing it, they use the information from a green ball to form their hiring decisions, and then they are surprised when their new hire doesn't behave as expected.

Behavior-based interviewing requires that actual past behaviors are used. This is good because real examples are better than hypothetical responses. But it still doesn't tell us how to distinguish between the consistency of behavior, what behavior is predominant, or how to see the color of the example. Although behavior-based interviewing is more effective than hiring strictly from gut feelings, it's still not enough to gauge a person's future job performance.

Pre-employment testing, another advancement in hiring, was designed to aid interviewers in identifying high performers, not replace them. When interviewers lack the proper training, however, the outcome of the test is used to make the hiring decision. The problem with this is that tests are typically not 100 percent accurate. I have personally validated a pre-employment test that turned out to be only 27 percent accurate (or 73 percent inaccurate) at predicting good hires. Let me put that into perspective: a flip of a coin would have produced better hiring results than that test. I am not against preemployment tests. I am simply for validating them; otherwise, we could be hiring underperformers and needlessly turning away great hires. First and foremost, the spotlight must be on the interviewer's skill level and how to improve it.

Quality-of-Hire: Why Isn't It Being Tracked?

When we analyze our hiring effectiveness, all we are able to do is examine the performance of candidates we have hired; we have no means to compare the performance of candidates we hired against those we did not. In truth, we don't actually *know* whether the best candidates are being hired. All we know is how the candidates who we hired are performing. Organizations must go beyond just tracking hiring *efficiency* using metrics such as cost-per-hire and time-to-fill. These metrics alone suggests that a fast and cheap hire is the most important measure of success, while actual job performance is irrelevant. Using this would be like imitating a factory assembly line that focused solely on the speed of output with little emphasis given to the quality of their product.

Quality-of-hire metrics, on the other hand, reveal the *effectiveness* of the employee selection process, as well as the effectiveness of the hiring managers. Unfortunately, it's not something I'm seeing a lot of organizations track yet. This means most don't really have a clue about how well they are doing when it comes to hiring high performers. The real purpose of these metrics is to trigger-positive change. Absent of that knowledge, there is usually no motivation to improve hiring results. I see two common reasons for inaction. The first reason is that no one seems to know exactly how to do it. The second is that it hasn't been made important enough to be mandated. It's part of the big picture of the state of hiring.

For organizations that are ready to get out of the Dark Ages, I've created a great tutorial on how to track quality-of-hire. It's easy, effective, and free. It includes a downloadable Excel spreadsheet with the formulas already built in and simple step-by-step instructions. To find it, visit the Hire Authority website and look for "Tutorial—How to Track Quality-of-Hire" under the "Free MBI Resources" menu, or go directly to it at www.hireauthority.com/qoh.

Better-Educated Job Seekers

In the United States, the Great Recession began in December 2007 and ended in June 2009, according to the US National Bureau of Economic Research, the official arbiter of US recessions. During those nineteen months, close to nine million jobs were lost and those interviewing for available jobs were desperate for competitive tips. The Internet became a historically unprecedented platform for an abundance of information on how to ace job interviews. Articles and videos offered good advice on what to do and what not to do in order to impress interviewers, and it was all available at the touch of a finger.

Regardless of the labor market, no candidate wants to be rejected. To maximize chances of a job offer and minimize rejection, all candidates must market themselves by accentuating their positives and minimizing their negatives. This paradigm makes it challenging for interviewers to gather relevant candidate information. To make matters more challenging, interviewers typically have a limited time period to gather the information they need to make quality hiring decisions. Some interviewers inadvertently set up their candidates or themselves to fail by mishandling the interview. For instance, an interviewer who talks too much learns less about their candidates, and interviewers who give away too much information up front unwittingly disclose to the candidate precisely what the interviewer would like to hear. When it comes to information gathering, neither of these tactics are effective, although both are commonly practiced.

Candidates are on their best behavior and many have even prepared and practiced answers that show off their successes. A close friend recently shared several experiences she had as a candidate with the popular interview question, "Tell me about your weaknesses." She said that the first time she was asked this question, she answered it honestly, spilling damaging information about herself. Later, after reading articles on how to land a job and after gaining additional interviewing experience, she learned to provide answers that actually diverted attention away from her weaknesses. Instead of mentioning that she usually runs late, she stated that she is a workaholic who sometimes has trouble juggling everything she is trying to accomplish. She further added comments about how she has improved herself by finding better ways to get more done. All of this was a prepared marketing strategy to avoid divulging her actual weaknesses.

Candidates are learning more about getting a job than the interviewers are learning about hiring well. It means candidates are becoming better educated at interviewing even though they're not good hires. It's time to even the playing field. Better yet, it's time for someone to give the advantage to the interviewers. Only when interviewers learn how to identify and hire genuine high performers does everyone win; bad hires are a serious problem for organizations, but it's certainly no picnic for the bad hire either.

Motivation: The Missing Piece of the Hiring Puzzle

When it comes to hiring, in order to gain a complete understanding on why much of what we're doing is broken, we must also address the topic of how interviewers assess a candidate's motivation.

> **Motivation is the energy employees invest in their work.**

First, it's helpful to understand a few things about motivation. Motivation is the energy employees invest in their work. How motivated a candidate is to do a job doesn't always equate to what they say or imply during an interview. Most, if not all, candidates will profess to being highly motivated. Well, we know *that's* not true. Motivation assessment commonly goes awry because interviewers assume that if they see any signs of initiative or drive, however small, their candidate is self-motivated. This perspective views motivation as being binary—either on or off, there or not there. It fails to measure motivation in degrees, or realize that there is no such thing as zero motivation. That means every candidate, including (or particularly) low performers, can provide at least one example of a time they were motivated. This makes it hard to distinguish the genuine high performers from everyone else.

Another common misconception about motivation assessment is that if someone is highly motivated to do one job, then that person will also be highly motivated to do any job. This isn't true— people are more motivated to some things and less motivated to do other things. Employers leverage motivation by tapping into what motivates a person the most and then placing them into a job that matches. This is how the energy of motivation gets funneled into the job. Interviewers who get this wrong often try to talk employees into loving a job they don't. It's akin to putting a square peg into a round hole and then trying to convince the square peg to be round, rather than hiring a round peg in the first place.

The customer service industry is a prime example of hiring gone wrong. Poor customer service is at epidemic levels. That's because people who don't like to serve customers are hired and placed into customer service jobs, and no amount of training or motivating will fix what interviewers miss. Realizing that motivation assessment is the key to hiring well isn't a new concept. Understanding that neglecting this assessment is the number one reason why most hit-and-miss hiring occurs and knowing exactly how to fix this problem is a new way of thinking for many.

The Next Evolution of Interviewing

Most interviewers just want to hire well; they don't want to devote their careers to studying interviewing techniques. For me it's different. I have a passion for hiring. I was tremendously excited to discover the significance of motivation assessment as it relates to hiring, to clearly see the holes in the employee selection process that allow marginal job performers to slip through (as outlined in this chapter) and to know exactly what to do to close them. I felt like a scientist who had found a cure for a disease—okay, maybe not quite that dramatic but exciting and hugely impactful just the same. I knew it was time for the interview to evolve. Motivation-based interviewing (MBI) was born.

Few realize that behavior-based interviewing, introduced by an industrial psychologist, wasn't an instant success. It took about twenty-five years before it became common practice. As I am writing this, MBI is turning twenty and it's catching on like wildfire. For those of you who are not yet familiar with it, MBI is an interviewing method specifically developed for hiring high performers that's been validated and is being used around the globe. It assesses the three components all high performers share in common: *skill*, *attitude*, and *passion*. You will learn all about MBI in the chapters to come. There are a number of methods available to learn MBI and improve interviewer proficiency, including an interactive online MBI web course, instructor-led workshops that are open to the public, and onsite training. To implement MBI throughout the enterprise, there's also a Certified MBI Trainer course available. For medium to large organizations, having a Certified MBI Trainer on-staff is a very cost-effective approach.

Before one can learn MBI, however, it's crucial to understand exactly how high performers achieve above-average results while others can't or don't. This understanding forms the foundation that MBI is built upon, so Part I of this book will cover it. Having a solid grasp of this foundation is an absolute necessity so that everything that follows will make perfect sense. Warning: If you didn't have your seatbelt buckled already, it might be a good idea to buckle it before turning the page!

Part I

Understanding High Performers

Chapter 2
The Process of Achievement

Let's look into understanding possibility versus impossibility and how a person chooses to believe one is true over the other. Is there a way to quantify and measure attainability? Is there a barometer that can measure feasibility? If no such device exists, then how do we know what to try and what not to bother with, and when to persist and when to give up? Well, this device actually does exist, but it's hidden in the human mind.

In order to hire well, we must understand exactly how high performers are able to produce consistently superior results. We must comprehend what truly sets high performers apart from everyone else. Here's a clue: it has nothing to do with a person's skill.

Think of achievement as a constant process that has unwavering and immutable laws that neither favor or oppose us. The road to achievement is impartial. Think of writing a computer program: it doesn't matter who writes the code, but if it's not written correctly, it's not going to work. The same is true with the process of achievement. The laws bend for no one. By operating in alignment with these laws, one can achieve superior outcomes.

Every goal—*every goal*—involves some degree of impediment that blocks the path to the desired outcome. These impediments are known by a number of different names: roadblocks, barriers, hindrances, adversity, challenges, problems, complications, hard times... the list is almost endless. In MBI, these impediments are called obstacles. Obstacles are a normal part of success. The first law in the process of achievement is: *there are always obstacles.* They exist for high performers and low performers alike. This may sound like a no-brainer, but for some people it's not. Low performers believe others were able to deliver better results simply because they didn't encounter the same show-stopping obstacles.

The second law in the process of achievement is: *only those who find a way to overcome the obstacles reach their goal.* You may have heard the saying, "Those who fail to find a solution only find failure." The secret to success is all about one's ability to come up with ideas that can be cultivated into viable solutions. Think about it. If we don't figure out a way to get to the other side of the obstacle, for whatever reason, then everything comes to a standstill. We remain right where we are. No further progress occurs. We don't achieve our goal, period.

What makes an obstacle difficult is clear: we don't know how to overcome it. The high performer doesn't know, and the low performer has no clue either. Initially, everyone is in the same boat. We must assess our likelihood of success by deciding whether an obstacle can or cannot be overcome before we know how. This assessment or prediction is crucial because it determines what we do next. If we conclude that we cannot conquer an obstacle, what we do next is—get ready—not much! We're not very motivated to achieve something we believe to be unachievable. On the other hand, if we think there is a glimmer of hope, that it is indeed possible to achieve our goal in spite of not having the solution at hand, that's when we become motivated to try.

It's this thought process that is *the most critical point* in the process of achievement. It's also the point at which the process of achievement most commonly breaks down. It's a fork in the road that will ultimately determine who succeeds and who doesn't. It's also the point where the high performers separate themselves from the pack.

> It's this thought process that
> is *the most critical point* in the
> process of achievement.

Attitude

This book defines "attitude" as one's tendency to think and behave in either a positive or negative manner toward obstacles. By adulthood, one's attitude has become established, and our response to obstacles is not much more than an unconscious, split-second reaction. When encountering an obstacle, people make up their minds very quickly as to whether it can or cannot be overcome. As we move forward through this book, you will discover the significant role that obstacles play in exposing a person's attitude.

Attitude is a powerful predictor of future performance and success. Attitude is so extraordinary that it dictates who enters problem-solving mode and tenaciously pursues a solution versus who gives up and quits trying. You don't need to be Albert Einstein to know which mindset will produce the better outcome.

To recap, every time a person encounters an obstacle, they must make up their mind about whether the obstacle can or cannot be hurdled. Only those who believe it's possible take the next step. For those who don't, they stop trying here. It's really that simple.

Up until now we've only been talking about the mental process of predicting the likelihood of success. Next, but only for the optimist, it's time to jump in and start the journey to the goal. It doesn't take long for the first roadblock to appear. This is where we normally begin to seek a solution, but not everyone will. According to Bruce Hinrichs, professor of psychology at Century College, thoughts are precursors of action, however not all thoughts produce action. Scientists have identified the frontal lobe as the region of the brain where problem-solving occurs. Interestingly, it's the same region that controls a person's motivation. Here's the most significant part: "I can" thinking switches on the problem-solving and motivation part of the brain. It lights it up! Scientists know this because of an invention of Paul C. Lauterbur and Sir Peter Mansfield, who won the Nobel Prize in Physiology or Medicine in 2003. It's called functional magnetic resonance imaging, or fMRI.

It's a big, magnetic, donut-shaped machine large enough to slide a person through. It has allowed scientists to watch the brain in action and track how it functions. It works by picking up spikes in oxygen use, which signal added activity in a particular part of the brain. That's where the description of the brain lighting up comes from. With "I can" thinking activating the problem-solving part of the brain and "I can't" thinking causing this part to remain dark and dormant, it seems that the human brain is wired to prove our attitude right. This is what makes attitude so significant.

The process of achievement doesn't usually involve a single obstacle, or even a nicely ordered line of obstacles. It can easily involve numerous obstacles that need to be dealt with concurrently. Innovation and out-of-the-box thinking are necessary ingredients for conquering obstacles. Creativity is the mother of invention. It's about expanding the mind in search of a solution and using every resource available. It's about whittling away at the obstacles until the envisioned outcome is created. But most importantly, conquering obstacles is about having the right attitude, because that's the ignition switch that activates the mind's powers. Without problem-solving, success cannot happen.

There is a third law in the process of achievement: *there is always a solution.* For some problems, a solution may not occur in one's lifetime—for example, finding a cure to a disease. It may not be cured today or tomorrow, but like many diseases, a cure is eventually found. Low performers have a tough time with this law. Their rationale for not trying is their belief that something is impossible in the first place so there can never be a solution. It's the belief that a solution exists that keeps a person in the game. The process of discovering a solution also involves plenty of trying and failing, and trying and failing, and so on. Thomas Edison said he failed more than ten thousand times trying to invent the incandescent light bulb. What mattered was that he never gave up. Defeat, setbacks, complications, disappointments, and an endless parade of obstacles with no apparent end in sight all test our resolve. In the process of achievement, perseverance is a must. The high performer's steadfast belief that a solution is within reach, often in the face of opposing points of view, is what keeps them engaged long enough to achieve the toughest of goals.

In many ways high performers and low performers are doing exactly the same thing. They are both using the process of achievement in exactly the same way—to produce what they believe to be possible. The difference lies in what each believes to be possible. It is this distinction that separates the two.

As you now know, there are three laws in the process of achievement: *there are always obstacles; only those who find a way to overcome the obstacles reach their goal;* and *there is always a solution.* Each law involves dealing with obstacles and is steered by a person's attitude. High performers have the kind of attitude that works in alignment with the laws. Low performers, on the other hand, work contrary to the laws of achievement through their insistence that obstacles eliminate any possibility of success. Obstacles only determine outcomes when we fail to try, fail to find solutions, or we quit too soon—all of which are controlled by our attitude. By understanding the process of achievement and working in alignment with its laws, every human being has the capacity to achieve great results.

We are just beginning to comprehend the powerful impact a person's attitude has on work performance, an impact that makes it one of the most important criteria for hiring, even more important than skill. A person's attitude is woven into every aspect of their life. It doesn't get left at home when they go to work. It goes with them. There is a direct relationship between a person's attitude toward overcoming obstacles and the level of effort that they will put forth. Similar attitudes can be found in similar performance levels no matter what the job entails. Now that we have a fundamental understanding about the process of achievement and how it works, it's time for us to dive deeper into our understanding of attitude.

"I Can" versus "I Can't"

Attitude would be better classified as positive and optimistic or negative and pessimistic instead of right and good or wrong and bad. A positive attitude refers to the "I can" or "it can be done" way of thinking. It is the type of mindset that is optimistic and open to considering all the possibilities. It is considered active because it spawns action. This attitude chooses to partake in the most hopeful view of matters and focuses on solutions. These thinkers conceive success and then get busy making it happen.

A negative attitude refers to the "I can't" or "it can't be done" mindset. It creates barriers and self-imposed limitations, and builds a case for why a goal cannot be achieved. It makes mountains out of molehills. This attitude is considered *passive* because it stifles action. This attitude is unhelpful, discouraging, and problematic. It blocks knowledge and even erects mental barriers to prevent success. Given the same set of circumstances, the positive attitude expands to think about possibility and opportunity, whereas the negative attitude squelches ideas and shoots down viable solutions. Both ways of thinking are common in most workplaces.

So, why can't people with a negative attitude who are filled with doubt produce just as much as those with positive attitudes? They may think they can, but they cannot. The mind is unable to act upon thought that is not present. When negative thought is occupying mental space, the focus is on why it can't be done, not on problem-solving effort and action.

Another distinction between attitudes is that the "I can" attitude believes first. It can visualize the desired outcome before it happens. These people achieve because they spend time thinking about how to do it. The "I can" belief empowers its owner and activates self-motivation. The "I can't" attitude needs to see proof before believing that something is possible. The thought and the belief that something can be done must come first. NASA succeeded at putting a man on the moon because they believed it was possible. As astronaut Edgar Mitchell stated, "Mass is merely dense thought."

For example, before a table could exist, it had to be conceptualized. It had to be sketched out and designed. The flaws had to be worked out and someone had to be motivated to stay with it for long enough to turn the idea into a physical reality. This is the dense thought and intense focus that goes into achieving every goal. The table, or mass, is the result of the dense thought. The thought and the outcome are a continuum; they are one and the same. Our belief in what is possible becomes a self-fulfilling prophecy. We act accordingly to make our beliefs a reality, whether we realize that we are doing this or not.

Let me use a computer as an analogy to make another point about attitude. Think of attitudes as being the software programs that operate the computer. Well-written software, akin to the "I can" attitude, optimizes the capability of any computer. Poorly written software, such as the "I can't" attitude, wastes processing power and diminishes the capability of the machine. The point is that while a computer may have the raw power to do many things, the program that's running ultimately determines what the computer will or will not actually do. Attitudes can likewise enable and disable people. High achievement requires a better program.

Failure

The first unmanned rockets exploded or went off course countless times before its inventors got it right. Abraham Lincoln lost almost every election prior to being voted the president of the United States. As Thomas Edison said, "People are not remembered by how few times they fail, but by how often they succeed. Every wrong step is another step forward." He also said, "None of my inventions came by accident, they came by work." Adversity tests the strength of the

"I can" attitude. It filters out those people who are not yet willing to do what it takes. You can tell a lot about a person by how they respond to failures.

You should realize by now that believing that you can accomplish something is a determining factor toward putting forth continual effort. Just as the saying goes, "If at first you don't succeed, try, try again!" Obstacles don't force a person to give up; on the contrary, they can be great learning opportunities. Failing many times before succeeding is common. Failure provides information that can be beneficial to discovering what does work. The lyrics to the popular song "Never Surrender" sung by Corey Hart state, "No one can take away your right to fight and to never surrender." Failure occurs only when one gives up. Quitting guarantees failure every time for every person, without exception.

On the Apollo 13 space mission, everything possible was going wrong for NASA. The oxygen supply was nearly depleted and the carbon dioxide filtering system was about to fail. NASA had no way of knowing whether the heat shields necessary for a safe re-entry were damaged during an explosion. The space agency didn't know whether the parachutes required to slow the spacecraft to a safe speed for splashdown would deploy. There was even a typhoon brewing in the ocean where the astronauts were to be picked up. In the movie *Apollo 13*, a NASA employee is overheard saying, "This could be the worst disaster NASA has ever experienced." Never giving up, Gene Kranz, the director of flight operations (played by Ed Harris), speaks up: "With all due respect, I do believe that this is going to be our finest hour." And against the odds, the astronauts returned safely home. Gene Kranz still gives motivational speeches with the tagline of his film counterpart, "Failure is not an option!" That's the kind of person you want to hire—someone who believes a solution can be found for everything, no matter how impossible it may seem.

"If Only... "

Pessimists focus on the negative aspects of their lives: a bad childhood, personal losses, traumatic experiences, past failures and struggles, fears, and self-pity, often caused by what others have done to them. And it is not just past wounds that get attention; they want to emphasize what is currently bad or wrong in their lives too.

Dwelling on negative aspects of one's life doesn't exclusively belong to those who lack common sense or intelligence. IQ does not determine attitude. It is sad how many smart people get caught up in this kind of negativity without realizing how it needlessly weighs them down and holds them back. Underachievers believe that their particular obstacles or hardships robbed them of success. "I could have been a better teacher if only I had better students" is one example of "if only" thinking, and so is the thought, "If only the hardships had not happened, I could have achieved more." These explanations usually sound quite convincing coming from an individual who is in total belief. Many negative thinkers often complain about their hardships in hopes of being viewed as being at a disadvantage. Others assume the role of a silent martyr. Pessimists often garner polite sympathy from other people, which in turn fuels their negativity and enables their ineffective approach to difficulties.

Changing Attitude

Even though a person's attitude can change, it is up to the individual who owns it to change it. I am unaware of a way to successfully effect permanent change in another person. What a great solution that would be, though—hire anyone and then change them into whomever you want. Changing one's own attitude has to be a personal and willful choice.

It's not easy to break the habit of thinking a certain way over a lifetime, not just because it has become an unconscious habit, but also because it is a way of thinking one believes to be true and correct. Many people with an "I can't" attitude are likely not cognizant of it because they don't see their attitude as being negative. They see themselves as being realistic. There is significant resistance from within when it comes to changing one's attitude.

Although a change in attitude can dramatically improve one's life, that doesn't seem to be enough to facilitate change. It requires a serious commitment. It requires belief and desire. It must be sought after and embraced by the individual. Any such change must come from within. It's not something you can force another person to do. Sadly, the people who need an attitude adjustment the most don't see it. Rather, they believe it's the obstacles along with everyone and everything else that's in need of change, so much so they can't understand why everyone doesn't grasp that. With this mindset, permanent change will not take place.

In the Workplace

If we want employees who will achieve great things, we must hire people with an effective attitude. It's never a good strategy to hire people with the wrong kind of attitude, but it happens all the time. Motivating the unmotivated (or engaging the disengaged) is what organizations resort to when they get the hiring process wrong. It wouldn't be such a big deal if it actually transformed low achievers into high achievers. But it doesn't. Even if it provides some immediate relief, that's only temporary. It's not as if we can light a fire under an unmotivated person once and then we're done. *That fire must be kept lit,* because that person isn't self-motivated. By unsubscribing to the notion that we can maximize performance by motivating the unmotivated, we can finally move to a place where we can actually achieve maximum success.

Hypothetically, even if it were possible for an organization to change an employee's established attitude (which it's not), it wouldn't be feasible because of the cost, time, and resources required for such a monumental undertaking. Employers would have to become experts in human behavior, even more so than psychologists. Employees would have to undergo a change in thinking every time they made a job change to fit their current employer's needs. It would be a training department's nightmare! So, here's the general rule: *the attitude hired is the attitude that remains.* That means hiring someone with the right attitude should take priority— even over hiring someone with the right skills—because skill, unlike attitude, can be changed after the hire.

One more thing. Even though we all seem to be able to distinguish both good and bad attitudes in others, we tend not to be able to comprehend the self-imposed limitations of our own attitudes. However, if we were truly objective, and we determined that our own attitude was indeed deficient, it's doubtful we would choose to share this information with a prospective employer during a job interview. The candidates that we interview are no different. That means the job of assessing a candidate's attitude is solely the responsibility of the interviewer.

As we move on to Chapter 3, we're going to look at attitude and its connection with perceived control.

Chapter 3
Attitude & Locus of Control

When I was a little girl, somewhere around age five, my dad let me steer the car. We were on this dirt road where it was safe. I did pretty well going straight, but up ahead I was going to have to turn onto another road. The road we were on was coming to an end, and there was a big pile of dirt straight ahead. I didn't think I could successfully steer the car around the corner, and I was terrified I would crash into the pile of dirt. I didn't want to be responsible for that, so I threw my hands up in the air, closed my eyes, and refused to steer anymore. I bowed out! I mentally abandoned control and gave it away. I believed if I wasn't steering and the car crashed, it wouldn't be my fault.

People of all ages encounter obstacles every day, and choose not to try because they don't believe they can succeed. They throw their hands up or close their eyes. They just let things happen. They deny having power and insist that they're not responsible for how things turn out, a very unproductive attitude. At age five, I was not concerned with whether my thinking was productive, but neither are most adults.

Perceived Control

So, here's the question: Does abandoning effort and leaving an outcome to fate mean we have no control and hence no responsibility? This means a person passively sits back and waits for an outcome to unfold, leaving the actual outcome in the hands of someone or something else. The issue is not that fate possesses control, but rather that control has been relinquished. Denying control does not diminish the control we actually have, it just renders it useless. We cannot use the power we have if we don't believe we have it.

How much personal control a person believes they have is a perspective that clearly differs from person to person. Passive "I can't" thinkers believe that whatever happens, happens, and the outcome is out of their control. If this thinking is correct, then shouldn't whatever is believed to be in control—be it fate, luck, coincidence, parents, a boss, or other people— affect everyone equally? Does no one have personal control and choice? Do some have it while others don't? Or is it possible that everyone has control, but not everyone *comprehends* it?

When an obstacle or an undesirable situation blocks one's path, it's the attitude that "I can succeed anyway" that creates a sense of power that we can shape the outcome into what we want it to be. This is called *perceived control*. One's attitude can either give us a sense of power or take it away from us. Perceived control is invisible to most people most of the time. We can't see whether we have it or not. We don't see what we do with it—we don't even think about it, because it's become habitual behavior. We don't equate trying or not trying with our thoughts about perceived control. Typically, we don't associate our successes and failures with how much power and control we feel we either have or lack. In fact, it's much easier to analyze someone else's perceived control than it is to see our own. Having knowledge about perceived control does not make it easier for a person to see their own power or to recognize when it's been relinquished. Recognizing one's power takes intent, conscious effort, and introspection. One cannot fake a sense of perceived control by merely having knowledge on the topic. That's good news for interviewers, because it means you will be able to see your candidate's perceived control.

Control is a very interesting topic. With control comes responsibility. Taking control of something means accepting responsibility for the outcome, good or bad. Many people don't like taking control because they are unwilling to take responsibility for their failures. They deny control and place blame elsewhere to avoid being responsible or being held accountable. Sadly, many managers buy into this notion of being powerless and accept it as a legitimate reason for substandard job performance and poor results. In other words—people get away with it. And the cycle continues....

Locus of Control

Locus of control is the science behind attitude. It is a behavioral psychology dedicated to the study of perceived control and self-efficacy—the power to produce intended results. In the book titled *Locus of Control*—written by one of its founding psychologists, Herbert Lefcourt—Herbert states, "Whether people believe that they can determine their own fate, within limits, is of critical importance to the way in which they engage in challenges."

Locus is Latin for "location." Locus of control is about placement of control, or where control is believed to reside. There are only two locations of control. If people see themselves as possessing the power to conquer obstacles and thus able to achieve their goals, control is believed to be *internal*. People who think they are unable to overcome the obstacles believe the control over the outcome belongs elsewhere, with the obstacles or someone or something other than themselves, and therefore *external*.

An internal locus of control is also referred to as being internally motivated. It is associated with the optimistic "I can" attitude and is linked to self-motivation. An external locus of control is also referred to as being externally motivated. It is associated with the more pessimistic "I can't" way of thinking and is linked to lack of self-motivation.

Locus of control is connected to the amount of participation or effort that a person's mind will pledge to achieving a goal. Attitude and action, as well as achievement, are all linked to perceived control.

Where one person sees possibility the other sees impossibility. Both may feel strongly about their position. Both may present a convincing argument that their way of thinking is correct. Both will be right because only one of them will put in the necessary work to prove the goal can be achieved.

Think of perception of control as a doorway with achievement on the other side. The person with the positive, "I can" attitude sees an open door. The open door is symbolic of an opportunity that is available to that person because it is believed to be attainable. Those who think "I can't" or "it can't be done," see a closed door or no opportunity available. Locus of control is built around these two opposite perspectives.

Locus of Control Scale

Locus of control is measured on a vertical scale that consists of internal motivation on the top of the scale and external motivation on the bottom (see Figure 3.1). The scale is symbolic of the degree to

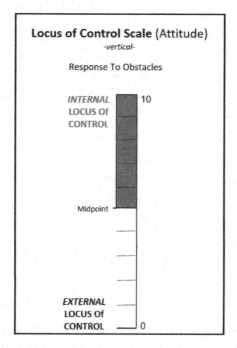

Figure 3.1. The Locus of Control Scale

which a person is self-motivated. At the top of the scale is ten, which represents 100 percent internal motivation. At the bottom of the scale, zero represents the inability to self-motivate, with sole reliance on external factors to push or cause motivation. Both a zero and a ten on the locus of control scale are theoretical since no one is purely one or the other. Even a couch potato will get up off the couch to replace the batteries in a remote control, placing that person above zero on the scale. My personal estimate is that most people score somewhere between three and eight, a few points on either side of the midpoint.

In the Beginning...

It seems that adults who faced *and learned to overcome* adversity in childhood are more resilient when encountering the obstacles and setbacks involved with achieving goals. Learning to deal with adversity during childhood instead of being protected from it has significant benefit. The overly protective parent robs a child of the opportunity for the practical learning experience necessary to prepare them for adult life. Sheltered children often grow up ill equipped to confidently and successfully deal with life's challenges. In the work-place, such exposure to adversity and obstacles is inevitable.

Babies seem to have a natural instinct to step into challenges and not give up. Learning how to walk is a perfect example of the process of achievement. Once a baby is ready to move from crawling to walking, what always happens? They all fall down, but they don't stay down. They get back up and keep trying until they conquer the challenge and master walking. If they didn't, we would have adults still crawling on all fours. At some point, however, some children learn to give up. They fall off a bike and never get back on. They don't learn how to swim. They're told all the things they can't do. According to many psychologists, there are multiple factors that influence the development of a child's locus of control, but by age seven it is 80 percent formed.

Entitlement Mentality

Saying you want something is not the same as saying you're willing to work to get it. For many, the preference would be to skip the process of achievement and have success handed to them. Entitlement is the perception or attitude that a person is owed the results of success without the need to work for it. It is associated with the external locus of control.

Vidal Sassoon said it so well: "The only place where success comes before work is in the dictionary." For the lower performers, their unwillingness to consistently do what it takes manifests from their powerless and pessimistic attitude: "Why bother, because there's nothing that anyone can do about it. It's impossible!" Through their eyes, the world operates on an unfair system controlled by other forces rather than on a system that rewards effort and persistence. In fact, effort and persistence are believed to have little to do with success at all. The fact that *they* bailed out is not viewed as affecting the outcome. Since they believed that they did not have control over the outcome in the first place, their choice of action was of no consequence. They were just responding to the inevitable outcome.

Victim Mentality

In the Eagles's song "Get Over It," the lyrics criticize the victim mentality so prevalent in today's society. Those who are familiar with the song know that it describes the way many people complain about life. These complainers see themselves as the victims of everyone and everything imaginable yet assume responsibility for nothing. The feeling of powerlessness parallels feeling like a victim. Externally motivated people focus outward on what others do to them, an area they cannot control. They don't focus inward on their own behavior or on what they *can* do and *can* control. Internal control is not really missing in people who are externally motivated, but they can't see it because they're focused on what was done to them as opposed to what they can do about it. As discussed, outcomes are indeed determined by someone or something else when a person relinquishes control. This, in turn, reinforces the "I'm powerless" thinking and the cycle repeats.

This is not to imply that people always or never feel helpless. Self-motivated people can certainly feel helpless at times but tend to rebound better. Control-deficient thinkers, however, often insist they've tried everything when they really haven't, or they eliminate all possible options involving what they can do. They place victim status on themselves. Their view or focus shifts away from their own control and onto that of the outside world controlling them. This is the point at which control is relinquished.

Excuses, Excuses, Excuses!

To conveniently deflect responsibility, comedian Flip Wilson's character Geraldine Jones would always say, "The devil made me do it!" He made it humorous, of course. When the "external" (as we'll call an externally motivated person) blames circumstances and situations for their lack of results, however, it's not funny, especially in the workplace. They and their results are often unreliable. When an employee substitutes the desired outcome with an excuse, the organization suffers.

Excuses and results have an inverse relationship. There is no need for both at the same time; it's either one or the other. If the intended goal is achieved, an excuse is not necessary. But when the outcome falls short of the goal, excuses are frequently served up as a substitute. More excuses equals less achievements and vice versa. Who will gain more results, the employees with more excuses or fewer? The answer is the employees with fewer excuses, of course.

Excuses are designed to shift blame off oneself and shed responsibility: "It's someone else's fault, not mine. There was nothing I could do about it." Eventually, excuses become a habit. I remember interviewing a young man who wanted to get promoted and move up the ladder. During the interview, he expressed that he thought this was impossible with his current employer and that was why he was job hunting. He said that even though there were promotional opportunities available, the employer was selecting only women. By his account, the company was on a mission to have more women in management. Under such circumstances there was no possibility of promotion, so why should he bother trying? He may as well look elsewhere. This was his thinking.

Let me tell you what else came out in the interview. He wasn't reaching the company-set goal for profits, but that wasn't his fault. As he explained it, sales numbers were down company-wide, and he couldn't do anything to change that. There were things he could do to improve his job performance, but he always had an explanation for why he hadn't or couldn't. If he tried to make improvements at all, he couldn't have tried very hard. Perhaps this candidate is starting to sound like an easy no-hire, but his image was sharp, he was personable, the labor market was especially tight in his industry, and he had great work experience. Some good companies had hired him previously. But once on board, he wasn't getting promoted—and according to him, it had nothing to do with his ability. It was clear to me that this person wasn't a high performer. He had one excuse after another for why he couldn't accomplish results. He was completely unaware of how he was coming across because he thought his excuses made perfect sense.

An excuse is different from a reason. An *excuse* is designed solely to free a person from blame, fault, and responsibility. It is used to justify inadequate results or failure and most of all, to put the entire matter to rest. No more effort—that's it. It's just a defensive strategy to avoid being held accountable and mask any appearance of poor performance. After all, how can someone be held accountable when it's not their fault? At least that's what the person making excuses is hoping for.

A *reason*, on the other hand, is a sound analysis that draws a conclusion from fact. A reason is not designed to relinquish ownership of an outcome. It is designed to analyze the cause for the purposes of learning, troubleshooting, and mapping out a strategy to achieve the desired outcome going forward. It's about understanding what went wrong so we can tweak what we do next. In the process of achievement, it's the "try, fail, try, fail, try" part of the process. The most obvious difference is that an excuse is a substitute for results, ending the need for more action, whereas with a reason, effort continues toward achieving the desired outcome. Obviously, we want to hire people who get results and do not make excuses.

Common External Characteristics & Behaviors

It may seem strange that anyone who wants to achieve a goal would respond ineffectively when faced with challenges or would spend inadequate time seeking solutions. Unfortunately, we see it all the time. Once a person makes up their mind that an obstacle is insurmountable, they no longer have a reason to try. The reality is, however, that not trying at all or easily giving up looks bad. It may surprise you, but to the external, not looking bad is *very* important. Excuses, blaming, and complaining are tactics used to divert attention away from their ineffective behaviors such as giving up or refusing to problem-solve, self-motivate, or try, fail, and try again. They develop ways to camouflage their personal ineffectiveness. Some common external behaviors and characteristics include denying any wrongdoing, playing the victim, exaggerating the obstacles, negating solutions, and getting defensive, to mention a few. These are all common strategies they use to keep them from looking bad.

For externals, their results define them. If they fail, to them it means, "I'm a failure." When externals encounter obstacles, saying

"I can't" is how they get out of trying. If they don't try, they can't fail. At least that's the case in their mind, and it doesn't stop there. Externals have an arsenal of tactics designed to elevate themselves. To make themselves seem superior, they will attempt to make others appear inferior in some way. They plant the seeds of negativity, doubt, and limitation in the minds of others to undermine their confidence. They siphon the optimism, enthusiasm, and ambition from those who are willing to believe them. They take credit for achievements that aren't theirs. They are often quick to point out the flaws and faults of others, and may insult and belittle them as well. When an external gets called out, they deny everything and proclaim themselves the victim. They have mastered the art of concealing bad behavior while avoiding looking bad. In their mind, the less others achieve, the better they look. They don't want anyone to outshine them. Hire enough of these people and you will create a toxic culture that can paralyze any organization.

The Challenge Within

Think about how a person who cannot perceive their control views life. Put yourself in their shoes for a moment. If you're that person, you believe you're a passenger in life who can't do anything about where you are because you don't possess the control. When people say *you can* change your destiny, it's obvious to you that they don't understand the obstacles that exist in your life. If they truly understood, they would agree with you. You might say, "If I had the power to make things different, don't you think I would? After all, it can be very frustrating living a life that you can't change, so have a little empathy please! People who attained success obviously didn't face the hardships I've had to deal with. Life was easier for them."

Now imagine the tremendous shock if you realize that it's not *the world* that doesn't understand your hardships, but rather the other way around. It's you. Just try to wrap your head around the possibility that it is *you* who does not understand there is another way of thinking, a way you never learned that would produce better outcomes for you. Imagine how you would feel if you suddenly discovered that you actually have more power and control over outcomes than you thought, and that had you made use of it, your life would be much better. One of the toughest things to deal with would be the realization of the times when you mentally gave up without trying, blamed others, and made excuses, now that you know you *could* have done things to change the outcome. Your actions would have made a difference, but you didn't bother trying because you thought you were powerless. Now imagine the tidal wave of regret that would come with owning up to the responsibility for a lifetime of wasted opportunities. For many externals, they can't handle the truth.

Externals operate under two basic principles: Principle one is *do whatever it takes to not look bad*. Principle two is *don't change*. The need to change implies that they weren't right in the first place, which makes them look bad. Their egos shield them from the truth and keep them in the dark about the power and control they actually have. As a result, they resist personal change, miss out on growth opportunities, and become prone to repeating this cycle again and again. For these individuals, the actual challenge isn't about who or what out there is sabotaging their success. Their biggest challenge lies within.

Common Internal Characteristics & Behaviors

Unlike externals, internals are not defined by their results. When they fail, which they do, they say, "I failed." This in no way means *they* are a failure. If it did, it would mean all high performers are failures, since it's a normal part of getting to any goal. Not taking failure personally makes it easier for them to step into challenges and try, fail, try, fail, try, and fail again without their failures negatively defining them. They own their results, even their unsuccessful ones. It's through failure that we learn the most, but only if we're willing to learn. Internals are willing. They're also not easily discouraged. I like to call them resilient optimists. They get knocked down and they get back up. They get knocked down again and again and again… and they keep getting back up. They keep believing a good outcome is possible *even when others don't*. Their "I can" attitude is akin to the Energizer Bunny. It keeps going and going and going.

Internals are the creative problem-solvers. They don't deny the problems or get fixated on what went wrong. They get to work.

> Solutions are equally accessible to all, but they never manifest for the "I can't" thinkers because they don't believe solutions exist.

They start thinking and talking about finding a solution: "How do I move myself from here?" Have you ever noticed when you direct your brain to find a solution, it keeps working on it even when you're not consciously focused on it? At 3 a.m. when you're sound asleep, you can suddenly wake up in an "Aha!" moment, and the solution is clear. That's the power of the "I can" attitude. Solutions are equally accessible to all, but they never manifest for the "I can't" thinkers because those people don't believe solutions exist.

High performers are regular people who are simply more effective at the process of achievement. They believe in their power to create and they use it to overcome obstacles and achieve goals. Here's something that sets them apart: they can talk in specific detail about their actions and problem-solving efforts, because these details exist. That's not the case for externals. Interviewers can leverage this by learning how to use properly phrased questions that expose who does and doesn't have these details.

One of the most important benefits of internals is the positive effect they have in the workplace. These people aim high. Challenges motivate them to work harder. You've heard the saying, "When the going gets tough, the tough get going." It's the internals who are tough and get going. Most notably, they inspire by example. They encourage, uplift, and energize coworkers. They are a positive force. Internals are self-motivated, which means employee engagement tactics are unnecessary and will eventually become obsolete as more of these self-motivated high achievers are added to the payroll.

As we wrap up this chapter on internals and externals, it's crucial to understand that *every* human being, without exception, thinks both "I can" and "I can't" thoughts. In truth, no one is fully cognizant of all the control they possess. From time to time, everyone denies responsibility for their results, or rejects something that is actually possible. The question is, how often? In each person, one way of thinking and reacting to challenges occurs more often than the other. We'll discuss this in greater detail in upcoming chapters.

Chapter 4
Passion & Career Fit

If you think that because you have learned about the power of attitude, you know everything you need to know about motivation, you haven't yet. There's still more to come! Suppose you have a job opening where skills are not the deciding factor for hiring—for example, an entry-level job or a job that uses skills unique to your particular company. Or, what if you want to hire an intern or someone who wants to change careers? My point is that a proficiency in a particular skill would not be a factor in your hiring decision. In each of these cases, a new employee will require training, which requires an investment. How would you decide who to hire and invest in? Would you look for a person who has the right attitude for overcoming obstacles, a behavior common to high performers? If you find it in a candidate, do you think this will guarantee a high performer once you provide training? Many think the answer is yes, but that's not always the case. When it comes to hiring high performers, possessing the right kind of attitude is only one ingredient. The presence of an "I can" attitude alone is not enough to qualify a candidate as someone who will be a highly motivated self-starter after the hire. So, what's missing?

Let me use an analogy involving you, the reader. Let's say you have the right attitude and you believe you could become anything you want, including an astronaut. But what if becoming an astronaut is of no interest to you? Just because you believe you *can* become one doesn't also mean you *want* to become one. The same is true about becoming a surgeon, a police officer, or an accountant, if those professions do not interest you. Do you think your lack of interest would affect your motivation and job performance? Of course it would! Now let's go back to deciding whom to hire when skill is not a factor in the decision. Should we still assume that having the right attitude is all there is to high performance?

Road Trip

Imagine for a moment that you are in a car and on a road trip. This trip is called the road of life. Are you on the right road, going in the right direction? Do you have a destination? Are you enjoying yourself? Are you energized or are you exhausted? Would you rather be going in a different direction?

Many people start driving down the road of life without a second thought about where they really want to go. They jump behind the wheel and start driving in the direction the car is facing. Let's assume they could go anywhere they wanted. Can they say where that is? Are they heading in the right direction? After being behind the wheel for a while, anyone will acquire some driving skills. They learn how to negotiate corners smoothly, and speed up and slow down as appropriate. They encounter various road hazards, detours, and traffic. *That's true whether a person is going in the right direction or the wrong one.* You're probably thinking, "So what? Driving is driving, right?" But that's not the case at all. On the road of life, it's not just about having driving skills. Traveling down the road that's right for you is what matters when it comes to being highly self-motivated.

When I'm teaching an interviewer workshop, to make a point, I often poll the attendees to see how many of them have had more than one career. Every time I've done this, a number of people have raised their hands. No matter how they got into their prior professions and no matter how long they stayed, every one has said that they eventually got out because they no longer enjoyed it. They were glad they made a change because they were then doing something they loved. These are capable people who admit they were no longer very motivated to do their old jobs. They wanted to do something that excited them and brought more fulfillment. It happened to me too. I was in a job I loved and got a promotion. This promotion took me out of a job I loved and put me into a job that was filled with the kind of data-crunching tasks that I absolutely hated. One Monday morning when the alarm clock went off, I hit the snooze button again and again. I asked myself, "When did I stop loving my job?" The answer was when I stopped doing what I loved to do. I left that company within two months. I wonder how many of the people who don't raise their hands in my class wish they were doing something different?

So, what does all this stuff mean—right road, wrong road, loving what you do or not? Why is it really so important that people love what they do and are excited or passionate about their work? Does it really make that much of a difference in job performance? The answer is *absolutely yes!* How motivated do you think a person would be to go above and beyond the call of duty if they had little interest or flat out didn't like doing their job? Ask this of yourself. From either angle, the answer is that they wouldn't be as motivated as a high performer. But why is this?

Interest forms a bond between a person and an outcome. Interest makes it personal. In the absence of interest, there is often indifference. Each of us has encountered someone in customer service who couldn't care less about us as a customer. Conversely, someone who has a vested interest in delivering the best possible outcome does it *because they care*. The children's song "Hokey Pokey" describes it well. One part of the song goes, "You put your whole self in, you take your whole self out, you put your whole self in and you shake it all about... and that's what it's all about." The weaker the interest, the less a person puts their whole self in. The greater the interest, the greater a person puts their whole self in. This is the same as giving it your all. High performers give it their all and low performers don't.

Right Road or Wrong Road

Many factors outside of our personal interests influence early career choices: parental and social influences, economic conditions, the desire for money, the ease of the opportunity, and so on. The truth is that many people do end up in wrong professions, going down a road that's not right for them. This comes at a cost. This road never allows a person to unleash their full potential. The right road does.

> The truth is, many people do end up in wrong professions, going down a road that's not right for them.

The rewards are greater on the right road. It's a shame that so many people undermine their own potential and pay such a steep price with no awareness of it, all because they chose a career path that might have been fine for someone else but wasn't right for them. The good news, however, is that there are many who come to this realization and choose to correct their course. At that point, the penalties are lifted and their performance soars. High performers commonly attest to the fact that the key to their success was finding a career they loved, whether by seeking it purposefully or discovering it by chance.

Where Does It Come From?

How much do we really know about the role that interest level plays in motivation? Where do our interests come from? One of two schools of thought is that interest is just a strong inner attraction to a particular profession—no more and no less than a preference that we pick up somewhere along our way. In this school of thought, it's something some people have and others do not. Is it any coincidence that career attraction happens to correspond with our own natural talents, strengths, personal likes, and interests? The things that interest us also seem to be things at which we can excel. For those fortunate enough to have an affinity to their chosen vocation, motivation is limitless.

Another viewpoint held by many including myself is that we *all* have a calling in life. Our natural talents, strengths, likes, and interests are unique, God-given gifts and tools that are intended to help us fulfill our purpose. Think of it as specialized programming that each of us has been given. Those interests that motivate us function as a steering mechanism designed to direct each one of us to discover, develop, and deploy our special talents and strengths. In return, we experience the joy and satisfaction that come with doing something we love to do. We are fulfilled. God's purpose is not for everyone to become the next Mother Teresa; it's about using what we've been given to fulfill our part in the big picture, while having a positive impact on the people we touch along the way.

Have you ever noticed that we can't completely forget or ignore this inner voice that seems to steer us in a particular direction? Why do some refer to this inner voice as a *calling*? Is it because the only way to quiet it is to follow it, and we never feel entirely fulfilled until we do? The term *fulfillment* comes from the Old English word "fullfyllan," meaning to fill up or make full. We have a built-in navigation device that guides us toward fulfillment, not away from it. This inner voice encourages the re-examination and the righting of incorrect career courses. Following the voice inside may not be easy, but ignoring it never produces contentment. When interest is absent, it creates a void that yearns to be satisfied. The search for fulfillment often involves career counselors and career changes. It used to be called a midlife crisis, but now it is happening to adults of all ages. It has been said that the fear of aging belongs to those who have not yet found fulfillment but still want to.

Many words work well to describe this inner voice that guides everyone. You can call it interest, calling, cause, mission, fancy, inspiration, aspiration, ambition, dream, desire, motive, what sparks us, and so forth. In MBI, we simply call it *passion*. It is a powerful influence that energizes and produces a high level of self-motivation within us unlike anything else. We don't have to fully understand how it works or why it works. For whatever reason, it just does.

Passion

Passion is an energy and excitement within that needs freeing. Oprah Winfrey, TV host and wealthiest African American of the twenty-first century, said, "Passion is energy. Feel the power that comes from focusing on what excites you." Passion is a strong inner attraction, a preoccupation, even an obsession, and it inspires us to act. It is the most powerful natural self-motivator there is. Passion acts like a magnet, drawing us to whatever it is we are passionate about. It is an emotion that comes from the heart and is reserved for describing what a person loves. Passion is *what* motivates a person. It's what a person finds interesting and captivating, not boring or distasteful. It's about pursuing one's personal likes, not one's dislikes. It's what we give our attention, energy, and focus to, and as a result it's where we develop our greatest strengths. We set goals to align with our passion, not against it. Passion is the *motive* portion of the word "motivation." In MBI, passion is simply defined as a person's likes, strengths, and goals, because these three indirectly correspond to a person's passion.

The Boss

In the prior two chapters, we discussed the powerful role that the "I can" attitude plays in the process of achievement. It sets a person in motion to seek solutions, conquer obstacles, and achieve goals. The "I can" attitude does not work alone, however. It has a partner—or, better stated—a boss. This boss, big cheese, head honcho, or whatever term you prefer steers a person's self-motivation in the direction the boss wants to go. Meet the partner of attitude and boss of self-motivation: passion. Although attitude clearly plays a significant role in the high performer's success, passion plays a more powerful role.

Remember the analogy about attitude and the open or closed door in the last chapter? Let's take it a little further. If the candidate sees the door as open, symbolic of an attainable opportunity, the next question is, Will they choose to walk through this doorway? The answer is, Only if the boss wants to. Passion is a selfish boss. If it says, "No, I have no interest," it cuts off the action, effort, and self-motivation behaviors. It wants to do those things that interest it. It wants to go in *that* direction and it wants to do those things. The fact that someone is showing initiative and is persistent does not mean they will consistently apply these behaviors to any and every job. We must pay attention to what task a person is performing at the time they show initiative and persistence; it's a clue to that which motivates them most. If a person lacks interest, self-motivation will stall. That's because motivation doesn't just happen or occur randomly in any and every direction. Passion is the most influential portion of motivation because it regulates the direction of a person's self-motivation, meaning it releases motivation to do certain things but not others. Without an understanding of this, it's impossible to truly understand motivation or how to hire highly self-motivated people.

When you think of passion, do you think of someone who gushes emotion almost to the point of making a spectacle? Can you imagine a low-key, demure person having passion? Demeanor doesn't convey passion. I once worked with a geologist in the petroleum industry whose job was picking locations for future drilling sites. He was considered a top performer in his organization and was very self-motivated. Interestingly, this man had a passion for rocks, so much so that his vacations often involved visiting caverns. He was quiet and reserved, but his passion shone through.

Without exception, all people feel passionately about something, no matter how they personally express it. Passion is anything that an individual holds a very strong personal interest in. The outward expression of passion varies from person to person. It should, after all, because every person is different. An individual's passion points the way for that person and that person only.

Unfortunately, people don't always choose careers they are passionate about. Imagine having a career as a police officer or a surgeon when that really doesn't interest you. If using a gun or the sight of blood is not your cup of tea, it's going to negatively impact your self-motivation. My friend's father was pushing him to follow in his footsteps, become a plumber, and take over the family business. He tried it for a year before he found the courage to say, "No thanks" and then went on to become very successful in the insurance business, something that aligned with his passion. Not everyone who needs to make a course correction does, however.

Things that hold the least amount of interest typically go to the bottom of our to-do lists. For me, that's expense reports. They may be easy, and I have the intellectual capacity and skill to do them. It even makes sense to do them promptly in order to pay off the travel expenditures I've incurred. That doesn't change the fact that I hate doing them! I can't even talk myself into liking them. I understand how this process works, but knowledge doesn't help in this case—trust me. I still procrastinate! I put my expense reports off until I can't put them off any longer. I was never meant to be an accountant; I'd be miserable and anything but a high performer. Thank God there are people whose passion is accounting, such as one of my closest friends, who operates a successful accounting firm and absolutely loves what she does.

For a person's passion to be unleashed, it must have an outlet. But not just any outlet will do. Someone who is passionate about playing the violin needs to play a violin. A violinist without an opportunity to play never liberates their passion. The passion is still there, but stays pent up. The only way to release the powerful self-motivating force generated by passion is to do whatever it is that aligns with one's passion. Nothing else will do. The violinist cannot transfer their passion for playing the violin to a passion for data entry. Extra data entry training, a pay increase, accolades, or employee engagement tactics will not release the violinist's passion in the same way that playing the violin will unleash it.

Career Fit

There is no right or wrong passion. This means that when it comes to hiring, information about a person's passion is relatively meaningless in and of itself. It only takes on meaning when we compare a person's passion with the duties and responsibilities of a particular job. When a person's passion fits the duties and responsibilities of their job, it's called *Career Fit*. This is also when a job becomes the outlet for the candidate's passion. The energy generated by getting to do what we love gets funneled into the job. This reciprocating relationship provides an outlet for passion that is ready to take flight and for the self-motivated high performers to emerge from. It's a win-win situation.

Schools, outplacement services, and career advisers often use assessment tools or tests in an effort to determine the best type of job for an individual. One of the most common is called the Strong Interest Inventory. It does just what its name suggests—it inventories interests—but it does not stop there. This tool was originally developed in 1927 to assist military psychologists with the task of determining which recruit to assign to which job. It was recognized that a person who likes the job of cooking is different from someone who likes tending to the wounded or managing communications. The many benefits of finding a good match were already well known. Now, with the help of computer-based analytics, occupations are suggested by measuring an individual's vocational interests—their likes and dislikes. Over the years, this assessment tool has been updated and has evolved to keep pace with the changes in jobs. As a personal testimony, I can tell you that the Strong Interest Inventory accurately picked my perfect occupation. You should know, however, that career-assessment tools show us only one piece of the puzzle and that most were not designed for the purpose of pre-employment screening.

If you ever want to take a look at people whose passion and career are one and the same, just watch a video or read a book that profiles a high achiever. Oftentimes, the person being profiled will comment that he simply receives recognition for doing what he loves to do, or that she feels fortunate to be paid so well for merely following her dreams. High performers go after their dreams. Roadblocks and setbacks do not cause them to abandon their mission. They think about the obstacles just long enough to conquer them. They never take their eyes off their goal.

The existence of the right skill set or the mere presence of the candidate at the job interview is not an indication of passion or Career Fit. Even the presence of good skills coupled with a candidate's enthusiasm isn't a reliable predictor of Career Fit. Enthusiasm may be fabricated and can evaporate after the hire. A match occurs only when genuine interest is paired with the right opportunity.

It's important to note what Career Fit is *not*. It is not about fitting into an organizational culture. It's not uncommon to find organizations that make hiring decisions based on cultural fit. Personally, I do not believe this is a sound strategy for several reasons. First off, this mindset is where discrimination often hides: "If you're not like me—if you are different—then you don't fit in and cannot be hired." Moreover, if an organization is plagued with a culture of blaming, negativity, "I can't" thinking, or marginal job performance, hiring for cultural fit means hiring more of the same. It does nothing to improve the situation. No matter what your current culture is, you should be hiring high performers. High performers don't accept the status quo. They are self-motivated, out-of-the-box thinkers. Yes, they can be disruptive for a while—but in a wonderful way. Each job opening is an opportunity to hire someone who will outperform their predecessor. One by one, hiring high performers is how an organization's culture evolves into one that thrives, filled with passionate, self-motivated problem-solvers.

Career Fit Scale

Career Fit is measured on a horizontal scale that consists of passion to the far right and dislike to the far left (see Figure 4.1). Passion is the highest possible level of interest, whereas dislike is a lack of interest that extends beyond indifference to the point of thinking, "I really hate doing this job!" The Career Fit Scale represents the percentage of the job duties and responsibilities that align with a person's passion. It's unrealistic to expect a 100 percent match, as jobs are composed of a variety of duties and responsibilities. Ideally what you are looking for is someone who is passionate about performing the majority of tasks required to fulfill their role.

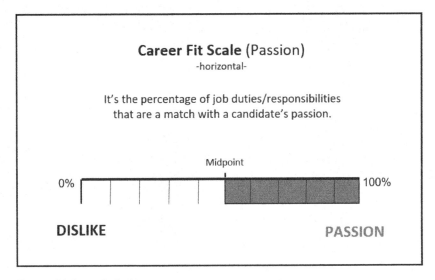

Figure 4.1. Career Fit Scale

Let the Rabbits Run

I love the opening story in the book *Soar with Your Strengths: A Simple Yet Revolutionary Philosophy of Business and Management* by Donald Clifton and Paula Nelson. It's titled "Let the Rabbits Run."[1] The story is about a rabbit, a fish, a bird, and some other animals who decide they want to become more well-rounded animals. They decide to go to school to cross-train in areas such as running, swimming, and flying.

You can imagine how the story goes. The rabbit does great in running. It's what he likes to do and also his area of natural strength. He receives lots of compliments on his ability and he likes going to school. He is energized and excited, and he wants to do more of what he does well. Now, imagine how poorly he performs at swimming and flying. The rabbit goes to his school counselor and says he no longer likes school because he doesn't like swimming or flying. The counselor replies by saying the rabbit is doing just fine in running and needs to work on the other areas instead. The counselor arranges for the rabbit to have two periods of swimming and flying and no running. When the rabbit hears that, he becomes physically ill! Outside, the rabbit runs into the wise old owl, who consoles him by saying that life doesn't have to be that way. He says that schools and businesses could focus on what people like to do and can do well. What a novel thought, concentrating on maximizing someone's strengths, not on a person's weaknesses or dislikes.

The rabbit naturally had the most interest in doing what he enjoyed and also could do well. Top athletes work on maximizing the areas in which they have the greatest potential and the most interest, all of which go hand in hand. It's the exact same principle high performers are using. Selling a person into liking something does not actually change their inner interests. If the job doesn't match what a person likes doing, even trying out the job won't make a difference. If it were to happen that the person did like the job, it's not because someone changed their interest in it but rather that the job matched their interests all along. Whether a person is aware of all of their interests or not, it doesn't change the fundamental principle that's at work here.

Passion, Time & Energy

It's amazing how a person's energy level and motivation bounce back once that person changes from doing something they find grueling or agonizing to doing something they love. This is because interest level regulates our energy and motivation. Disinterest drains energy and makes some tasks appear to require more energy to do. Time drags on. Procrastination is a common symptom of low interest. Small projects can look like huge mountains to those who lack the interest in them. A high interest level, on the other hand, creates an invigorated climber who is ready to scale any mountain to its peak. Interest is what keeps a person energized, engaged, and focused long enough to develop an advanced level of skill. A higher level of interest increases performance by dispensing more energy into behaviors that are more conducive to achievement. Can you see how motivation is enhanced through passion, and depleted by ambivalence or disinterest? A close friend recently shared her excitement with me about the possibility of starting a new magazine. The possibility energized her so much that she would wake up in the middle of the night with ideas on how to make it work. Despite having only three hours of sleep one night, she got up and worked on the project some more. Instead of feeling exhausted, as one might expect, she said she felt invigorated.

In the Old Days...

In the past, we put more emphasis on hiring for skill and very little emphasis on harnessing the passion that comes from doing what we love. In generations past, work was viewed strictly as a way to support the family and wasn't intended to be fulfilling. You went to work to earn a paycheck and sought fulfillment on your own time. But times have changed. We have evolved. The ways of prior generations don't apply to the workforce of today. People want to do work that's meaningful to them. It's likely that the high performers paved the way for this change. Their work was more like a hobby they got paid to do. Their preoccupation became their occupation, and like the geologist I spoke of earlier, their vacation became their vocation. They found their passion. They are energized and self-motivated as a result. You don't have to take my word for it, just ask any high achiever and they'll tell you.

Considering the amount of time we spend at work, we should be doing something we enjoy. Many have caught on to the magnificent feeling of fulfillment that comes with working on the very things they are passionate about. Imagine the difference between a day of work that was interesting and stimulating versus a day of boredom and exhaustion. There's no rule that says we cannot or should not enjoy our work. We affect other people in a positive manner when we're happy. Happiness isn't something that comes in the form of a paycheck. I've interviewed many candidates who were willing to accept a position with lower pay if it would give them an opportunity to fulfill their personal interests and goals. It just so happens that the most effective way to convince a candidate to accept an offer is to emphasize the aspects of the job that they expressed the most interest in during the interview.

No Substitutes

There is no substitute for passion. When a person is in the wrong job, both the employee and the organization suffer. Sugarcoating a job to make it look like something it isn't or like something the candidate will enjoy when his true interest lies elsewhere does nothing other than make a mess for everyone involved.

Worse yet, not everyone in the wrong job leaves. Many people who feel discontent with their line of work set themselves on auto-pilot and keep doing what they've always done. They just hum along, doing enough to get by but lacking the zeal that shifts a high performer into high gear. These people never become moti-vated enough to soar to greater heights. I remember talking with an owner of an HVAC company that employed about two hundred people. He stated that his office manager had been with him for ten years and had never done a very good job. When organizations get enough of these people onboard, this creates a *culture of mediocrity* where excellence becomes optional. Organizations often realize that they have a problem and use employee engagement tactics to try to solve it. Employee engagement doesn't work. Without addressing the root cause of the problem—how these low performers are get-ting hired in the first place—it acts as a Band-Aid at best.

The Skill Dilemma

Some people take their strengths and move them into a different career field. I know a person who was a professional musician for ten years, and then in sales for ten years, and currently has a very success-ful career in computer programming. He uses his skills in commu-nication and creativity to excel in his current profession, which he is passionate about. I remember when he first made the transition out of sales into the computer industry. It wasn't easy. High performers (or future high performers) chasing fulfillment may easily exist as candidates lacking the ideal set of skills.

Every day I encounter more and more people who express dis-content with their current occupation. In fact, that was the topic of conversation at a recent luncheon. The person I was speaking with said that the only work she has ever known was unfulfilling. She knew exactly what she wanted to do, but wondered if any employer would give her a chance since she lacked the skill. These people are often overlooked. There are future high performers out there who are seeking opportunity and hungry to learn. In a tight labor market, these candidates can be a great hiring option as long as you are able to correctly identify them and you are willing to train them.

Passion & Performance

I think most people generally acknowledge that matching a person's likes and interests with a job is good to do, but it's more than that. People need a playground or an outlet for their interests. When a job becomes the playground for passion, stand back! It's a win-win situation because both the organization and the employee reap the benefits. In the best-selling book *Good to Great: Why Some Companies Make the Leap and Others Don't*, author Jim Collins states, "We expected that good-to-great leaders would begin by setting a new vision and strategy. We found instead that they first got the right people on the bus, the wrong people off the bus, and the right people in the right seats."[2] Notice that he didn't say *transform* or *motivate* the wrong people into engaged employees. The passion-job match is all about getting the right people on the bus and in the right seats from the start. It's nonnegotiable if you want a high-performing organization.

Many of you already understand exactly what I'm talking about here: *the connection between passion and job performance.* I can hear you shouting, "Yes, absolutely yes!" Many others aren't able to relate to this message quite as well, however. They don't know because they have yet to experience it for themselves. It's not that they aren't one of the chosen few who have been allowed to experience passion. Rather, these people are either unaware that they should bring their passion to light and follow it, or they are aware but are unwilling to take that step. Some people start driving down the road of life without knowing where they want to go. Others don't even know that they're the driver—they believe they're a passenger. If you happen to be a person who never experienced the powerful feeling that comes from doing what you love, at least know that it exists.

Regardless of what path you choose for yourself, understanding passion and the powerful role it plays in the high performer's success is an essential concept you will need to fully grasp if you want to identify and hire genuine high performers. Many people, including many of the candidates you will interview, don't realize just how much passion affects job performance. People don't always search for jobs based upon areas of interest. It is only when an interest or passion that truly resides in the candidate's heart has the opportunity to be expressed in the position you are trying to fill that the highest level of motivation can emerge.

You've learned about the power of attitude and about the power of passion. In the next chapter we bring the two together.

Notes

1. Donald O. Clifton and Paula Nelson, "Let the Rabbits Run: A Parable," in *Soar with Your Strengths: A Simple Yet Revolutionary Philosophy of Business and Management* (New York: Dell Publishing, 1992): 3–8.

2. Jim Collins, *Good to Great: Why Some Companies Make the Leap and Others Don't* (New York: HarperCollins, 2001): 3–7.

Chapter 5
Motivation & High Performers

When a person's passion and "I can" attitude are strong enough, they will appear to have an almost superhuman ability to achieve. In this last chapter of Part I, "Understanding High Performers," we will unite the power of attitude and the power of passion, and understand exactly how it is that some people achieve exceptional results while others don't. Up to this point, interest level and perceived control have been discussed independently. Now we're going to merge these two concepts and see how they interact.

To review, a high degree of interest is labeled *passion*. Passion governs or steers effort. It is the *motive* portion of the word "motivation." It is *that which motivates a person the most*. It is what generates the highest level of self-motivation, in contrast to a low degree of interest, which saps energy. Interest pulls a person in and makes the outcome important. When there's no interest in something, it's as if a person is on the outside looking in with indifference about the outcome. To be highly self-motivated, an individual must have a high level of interest or a passion for what they are doing.

As further review, attitude is tied to perceived control and is associated with the suffix of the word "motivation" (-*ation*), which means "action," as in the action taken to achieve a goal. It is part of the behavioral psychology called locus of control, which is the science behind attitude. It is *how* a person is motivated—internally or externally. A high degree of internal motivation, or self-motivation, means a person has the ability to put oneself into motion. Those who lack internal motivation require a source other than themselves to motivate them. These people have an external locus of control. Locus of control is also the degree to which a person is able to self-motivate. All high performers have an "I can do it" attitude and believe *they are in control of their results.* This attitude is behind their ability to be highly self-motivated.

The Birth of Self-Motivation

Interest level and perceived control collaborate to produce varying degrees of motivation. Of the two components, can you figure out which one starts the ball rolling? Is it the stimulus from having a high level of interest? Or is it locus of control, specifically the "I can" attitude, a sense of being able to influence outcomes? Here's how it works:

1. A spark of interest awakens and activates the command center—"I want to do this!"
2. The program running in the command center (that is, the individual's locus of control) mentally determines whether taking action will yield a good outcome.
3. If the command center gives the nod—"I can do this!"—initiative awakens, effort is expended, and the wheels begin to move.
4. Interest steers action in the best direction to turn the passion into reality.
5. As passion and the "I can" attitude join forces, maximum problem-solving effort and persistence are summoned for the purpose of achieving the desired outcome. Combined, these two components create the highest level of self-motivation.

Each of the two components of motivation are continually assessed. Should either interest level or attitude wane, the behaviors associated with self-motivation are proportionally reduced. Note that problem-solving efforts and persistence are both always required to conquer obstacles and are the hallmark of high performers. When either or both of these ingredients is missing, forward motion stalls in the face of obstacles and the current endeavor is suspended indefinitely.

In step one, it was the spark of interest that got the self-motivation ball rolling. This stimulus starts out in command, but then locus of control takes over while processing possibility. Then it goes back to interest, the selfish boss that releases energy to satisfy whatever it loves doing the most. Motivation receives input from both interest level and perceived control and responds accordingly. The level of self-motivation that is generated depends on how much the right attitude and passion is present. At any point, if a lack of interest sets in, or a belief that an obstacle is insurmountable or a goal is unattainable occurs, self-motivation dissipates.

Two Scales Combine to Create Four Quadrants

In Chapter 3 we discussed the vertical Locus of Control Scale, with "internal" at the top of the scale and "external" at the bottom. In Chapter 4 you were introduced to the horizontal Career Fit Scale with "passion" to the far right and "dislike", or lack of passion to the far left. When these vertical and horizontal scales are combined, they create four quadrants that represent varying degrees of motivation (see Figure 5.1). Understanding these quadrants and how they differ will ultimately enable interviewers to distinguish incremental performance differences caused by varying levels of self-motivation. In other words, interviewers will be able to differentiate high performers from average and poor performers—and be right.

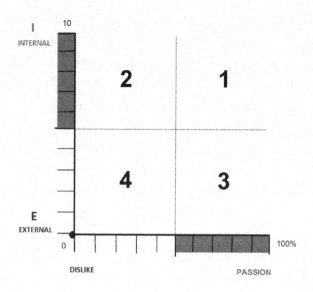

Figure 5.1. The four quadrants

Quadrant 1

"I can and I want to." You can almost feel the high level of self-motivation. Quadrant 1 is where internal locus of control and passion combine. It's the highest level of self-motivation generated by locus of control and by passion. Together it's like self-motivation on steroids. It's super self-motivation, the kind high performers have! Simon Sinek, leadership expert, said this about Bill Gates, who built the world's largest software company: "It's not Bill Gates's passion for computers that inspires us, it's his underlying optimism that even the most complicated problems can be solved."[1] This level of self-motivation is not reserved just for famous people. Ordinary people achieve extraordinary results in exactly the same way. This is what happens when these two forces combine.

For the employer, it's all about identifying and hiring highly self-motivated people and placing them in jobs they love, thereby harnessing the power of their optimistic, problem-solving attitude. When this occurs, the organization reaps the benefits of what these people produce. Self-motivation only decreases in the remaining three quadrants.

Quadrant 2

"I can but I don't want to." Right attitude, wrong job. If I were to use one phrase that best describes this average-performing quadrant, it would be "turnover waiting to happen." This can happen when interviewers unrealistically portray a job, leaving out the negative aspects. After being hired, some discover their job isn't quite what they were told it would be, and that it's not a good fit for them. In this scenario, you end up with employees who have the kind of attitude that takes action to solve problems, so they take action and solve the problem—by leaving. Passion acts like a glue; it has a sticky quality. Without it, there is nothing to hold a person in place when a job becomes frustrating. The reality is that every job has its frustrations. Having passion for doing the work increases tolerance levels. Organizations that experience high turnover (voluntary, involuntary, or both) are often hiring people and placing them into the wrong job. In addition to improving quality-of-hire, sometimes this can be resolved by moving people into other jobs within the organization that are a better match with what they love to do. A good example of this can be found in the food service industry. A server who struggles to provide satisfactory customer service but who has a good attitude and is reliable might be better suited for a job in the back of the house or vice versa. This may save an employee from being terminated, which is huge benefit in an industry that continually struggles with staffing.

Quadrant 3

"I want to but I can't." Right job, wrong attitude. This is a tough one. The term associated with this quadrant is "campers." That's because these average performers tend to pitch a tent and stay too

long. Campers like doing the work, so they have some motivation, but they have a powerless "I can't" perspective when they encounter tough on-the-job challenges. According to them, their mediocre job performance is no fault of theirs—and they believe this. To avoid being held accountable, they insist the goal was unrealistic and it was the obstacles that sabotaged their success. Sometimes these people can be toxic to an organization's culture by implanting doubt in others and undermining what's truly possible.

Quadrant 4

"I can't and I don't want to." With math, a double negative yields a positive result. In our case, however, this is a double negative that isn't a positive. These are not only people who have an ineffective attitude for overcoming obstacles, they've also been placed into jobs they don't like doing. They are the least motivated and the lowest performers, and no amount of employee engagement is going to fix what the interviewer missed. These people should not have been hired, period. Every day that you have someone filling a seat that could be occupied by a high performer, you lose productivity that can never be regained.

Most organizations have employee performance levels in all four quadrants. How did they get there? It's simple—they were all hired. The key to assessing motivation is to determine how much control a candidate believes they have to produce results *and* how much interest they personally have to do a particular job. High performers are people who possess a high degree of both internal motivation and interest. Conversely, the lowest performers lack self-motivation because they lack both perceived control and interest. *Both types of candidates,* along with the average performer in between, can interview well or poorly, have either strong or weak job skills, and be likable. Learning to correlate the components of motivation with job-performance levels will allow us, the interviewers, to see beyond a candidate's polished exterior and expose the information we need to choose the best person for the job.

Skills Aren't Motivators

Did you notice that skill was not represented in the four quadrants? That's because skills are enablers, meaning they *enable* a person to do a job. Skills are not motivators. They don't guarantee a person *will* do the job, or gauge how well they will do it. That's where motivation comes in. How self-motivated a person is or isn't is an indicator of the degree to which their skills will be applied. By the same token, it's important to understand that a person lacking skill can still be highly self-motivated. High performers can either have the skill to do a job or they can acquire the skill after they're hired, but they are also highly self-motivated. It's a combination of skill and self-motivation together that lives at the core of every high performer. All high performers share three ingredients in common: skill, attitude, and passion. These three key ingredients combined in sufficient quantity will produce the highest performance. Attitude and passion together determine motivation. Skills are not involved. A person with no skills can still be highly self-motivated.

Persistence and the Roles of Attitude & Passion

Without persistence, skill and talent go to waste. An employee who lacks persistence will never be a high performer. Conversely, lesser-skilled candidates can produce exceptional results simply by virtue of their unwavering determination. Successful people have a high degree of persistence. Employees whose performance is only average or lower frequently lack persistence.

Initiative, or taking the first step, does not guarantee success. Persistence is how long effort continues once motion has started. Without persistence, a person quits before achieving their desired goal, which reduces productivity. Persistence ensures problem-solving efforts keep going, which is fundamental to accomplishing goals. The level of persistence represents the degree to which productive action and effort toward reaching a goal is maintained.

Persistence corresponds to the degree of control a person believes he or she has. It's unnecessary when control over the outcome is believed to belong elsewhere. The greater the feeling of control, the greater the persistence. A bold "I can do it!" attitude produces relentless persistence in pursuit of a goal. A halfhearted optimistic attitude only produces a spurt of energy. This spurt of energy produces short-term persistence and nothing more. Conversely, a belief that something is absolutely impossible produces no perseverance, and often no effort whatsoever. Positive and negative thoughts each have a very different and profound effect one's level of energy. The fuel for persistence is the power of a positive attitude. Motivated people have the mental energy to persist.

Now that we've established that the power of a positive attitude influences persistence, what about interest level? Does it affect persistence, as well? *Absolutely!* Even with an "I can" attitude, if there is little or no interest, the energy won't flow. The selfish boss regulates energy flow. It also plays the role of fueling continued persistence. As long as there is continued interest, energy is released. If interest is lost, no further energy is released, and no energy means no persistence.

To summarize, persistence level is fueled by these two ingredients: A strong interest, or passion, and the level of perceived control over the outcome. Together, these two ingredients turbo-charge persistence. Here's how they interact: Think of locus of control as gasoline and interest level as a spark. Without the spark, gasoline remains a dormant liquid. It ignites the gasoline and also keeps the engine running. The gasoline is no longer in a dormant state—it is active. The spark from passion converts the "I can" attitude into a physical energy that is used to fuel self-motivation. High performers are energized. This energy is the driving force behind the high performer's self-motivation and persistence.

Just as the mind can giveth energy, it can also taketh away. When someone lacks self-motivation and fails to take action to achieve a goal, both perceived control and interest level should be checked. Does the person lack one or both? Has perceived control been relinquished and pessimism taken its place? Without perceived control, persistence will not ensue. Persistence is also suppressed when passion is lacking, however. It may well be that a person simply has no interest. Without this duo, the body may not be sufficiently fueled or energized to keep a person engaged in completing a task or achieving a goal. Absent of the powerful combination of interest and a positive attitude, performance will be average or lower.

Imagine everyone having the power to be just like Superman— to do remarkable work and soar to great heights. Now think of negative thoughts and the lack of passion as being like kryptonite, which depletes Superman's energy and drains his power. Some people carry around their own kryptonite, usually without realizing it. Drained of energy, unable to soar, they become mere mortals, capable of nothing more than average performance.

Learning Power

Some people repeat past mistakes because they never learn from them. They are on a merry-go-round of repeating experiences involving different people, places, and dates, but never moving ahead. They never learn what *they* are doing wrong or acknowledge what *they* could do differently to improve their results. They aren't aware of what they are responsible for or the role they play in creating their results. Despite lacking awareness of their own negative impact, they are easily able to point out the negative impact others have had on them. In their mind, they're always the victim and never the cause.

Learning from one's mistakes requires making the connection between one's actions and the outcome. In other words, a person's actions, or lack thereof, must be seen as contributing to whatever happens or doesn't happen. If it is not seen this way, then the viewpoint is that something other than oneself, something external, is responsible for the outcome. One may want better results but believe that can only happen when that which controls the outcome changes. Translation: *not me.* There is no need to change anything about oneself when an outcome is not one's fault; there's nothing to learn, so no learning takes place. This person thinks, "I'm not the one who caused this, so there's nothing I need to do differently." They lack an overall awareness of their own significance and effect. The end result is that they make the same mistakes over and over instead of seizing an opportunity to learn.

Who do you think fails more—high performers or low performers? High performers do—because *they try continuously.* They step into the try, fail, try, fail, and so on cycle that's a natural part of the process of achievement. They're not afraid to fail because failures don't define them. They view failure differently than low performers do. High performers treat failures as stepping stones and springboards on the path to success. They look at each failure as a learning opportunity and a challenge to be conquered.

A great example of this can be found in sports. American football quarterback Nick Foles had a disappointing season in 2015, followed by a short stint playing with the Kansas City Chiefs in 2016. Foles contemplated retiring from football altogether. After some serious soul-searching, in 2017, he signed with the Philadelphia Eagles, but only as a backup quarterback. He had been benched and turned into a backup, but then… he was resurrected. An opportunity arose, and against all odds, Foles led the Eagles to their first-ever Super Bowl win in 2018 and was named Super Bowl MVP (most valuable player). His biggest takeaway from it, he said, was to never give up on yourself. Foles added, "If something's going on in your life and you're struggling, embrace it, because you're growing."[2]

High performers don't avoid challenges; they aren't afraid to step into them and embrace them. Most importantly, they make the connection between themselves and their results and work hard to steer the outcome. They don't hold someone or something else responsible for their results, even though external factors may have contributed. They don't shed responsibility or place blame elsewhere. If high performers aren't producing the results they want, they ask themselves, "What am I missing? What am I doing wrong? What can I do differently?" It is this mindset that facilitates learning, personal growth, and best of all, success.

Lower performers often place the responsibility for learning on their teachers and blame them when they fail. If they have a difficult time at work, they often blame their employers for not training them sufficiently but never seek additional help. This shifting of ownership can occur regardless of whether they were sleeping in the back of the class or actively participated. They insist, "It's not my fault, I had a lousy teacher."

I remember an accounts payable clerk who was hired by the department manager. The new employee was trained and taught how to put department codes on all invoices and even had a reference book at her desk with all the department codes listed. For the codes she couldn't remember, rather than looking them up in the book, she would get up from her desk and ask her boss for the code. After retraining, coaching, counseling, and eventually disciplinary action, she was terminated three months after being hired. An exit interview was conducted. Her rationale for being let go was it had nothing to do with anything she did wrong. By her account, she was improperly trained, and her boss was unsupportive.

High performers may also struggle with learning, but they're apt to take control and do whatever extra work they need to do or action they need to take to overcome the situation. They take responsibility for their skill deficiencies rather than blame others for not teaching them. They seek mentors and do what it takes, even on their own time, to learn what they need to learn.

It's a night-and-day difference compared to how low performers react.

Learning is affected not only by perceived control but also by the other component of motivation: lack of interest, which can also contribute to lack of comprehension. What happens when you're trying to learn a topic you have no interest in? Your mind wanders because the topic can't keep your attention or focus. Some people actually cause disruptions in a classroom simply because they lack interest in the topic and they're bored. On the other hand, the opportunity to learn more about a subject that's of interest sparks our attention and awakens the senses. We transform into full learning mode. Someone who is genuinely interested and wants to learn a topic will do it, even if it involves extra effort.

Educators only provide the information. It is up to each individual to learn it. Training effectiveness is greater when those who are receiving the training have both an interest and take responsibility for learning. Learning reaches its highest peak when people are motivated to learn. When investing time, money, and resources toward employee training, having people with the right attitude and passion will produce the greatest return on the investment. It also helps the training department become more successful.

Environments: Are They Really to Blame?

Low performers who lack self-motivation will often blame their environment for demotivating them. They have no problem pointing out the imperfections and shortcomings in their employer and boss. They have a laundry list of external factors that robbed them of their drive. They've shed responsibility for their lack of self-motivation and make their employers responsible. Many employers have wrongly accepted the blame. This resulted in the birth of employee engagement, which ultimately made the use of motivational tactics the norm. Low performers insist that workplace imperfections have sabotaged their success. Let's talk about that.

A perfect work environment doesn't exist. Even if we could create it, we couldn't maintain it. It's impossible to remove all the challenges from the workplace and prevent any from occurring in the future. Whenever there are changes, for example a new technology being integrated into the workflow, employees are not going to know how to deal with it initially. That lack of know-how is a challenge in and of itself.

> **It's not the absence of obstacles that determines success.**

Hypothetically, even if we could create and maintain this perfect working environment, low performers would still conjure up new excuses for their lack of motivation, and not one of those excuses would lay blame on them. It's not the absence of obstacles that determines success. Believing the notion that people only operate at maximum performance when their working environment is obstacle-free means organizations are hiring people who are ineffective at the process of achievement. In the same environment where low performers are blaming the environment for their lack of self-motivation and success, high performers are motivating themselves and reaching their goals.

This doesn't mean organizations shouldn't create great workplaces that will attract and retain the best (after all, everyone likes a good workplace). When employers accept the responsibility for motivating the unmotivated, however, employees no longer need to be self-motivated. It means employees can get away with being unmotivated. Employers need to make up their mind who is responsible for employee motivation, the employer or the employee. They can't have it both ways. Realize the impact of the decision. One choice creates a culture of excellence while the other creates an "excellence is optional" culture. The whole concept of employee engagement enables and fuels the dysfunctional belief in an external locus of control. Not only do employers hire this mindset, they use employee engagement tactics to perpetuate it.

When A Cause Motivates

What one person perceives as a negative event or influence that nothing can be done about, another sees a reason, even a necessity, to take positive action. A negative event or influence can ignite passion and steer a person to a purposeful vocation. Depending on the person's locus of control, specifically if they are internally motivated, it can drive that person to fight for a cause and ultimately bring about monumental change.

The tragic story of a thirteen-year-old girl who was killed by a drunk driver with a lengthy prior record is an example of an external event that motivated people to take action. A group of women outraged by this tragedy believed their efforts could make a difference. They were right. In 1980, they formed Mothers Against Drunk Drivers (MADD) to stop drunk driving and to support victims of this violent crime. Today, more than thirty-five years later (and now known as Mothers Against Drunk Driving), the staff and advocates work tirelessly to support victims at no charge, advocate for stronger laws, and focus on the number zero: zero deaths, zero injuries, and zero families impacted by impaired drivers.

I'm sure there were those who felt nothing could be done about alcohol-related deaths because they had no control over other people's actions. The point is, the power to effect change starts with believing that our own actions can make a difference despite what others believe. Those who truly believe in their power to influence outcomes get further than those who don't. That's because they are the ones who jump in and try. They take on all of the obstacles that separate them from their goal. There are many examples of outspoken advocates who stepped into their roles as a result of some negative event or influence they experienced. The cause becomes their passion, and when merged with an unstoppable attitude, an incredible self-motivation is unleashed. It's the good that comes out of the bad. It's the light that shines through the darkness. The recent #MeToo movement is one such example. So is the #NeverAgain movement brought about by the tragic Marjory Stoneman Douglas school shooting in Parkland, Florida.

It doesn't matter how people find their passion. When they do, and when it's combined with the optimistic belief that anything is possible, that's when great things start to happen.

Who Doesn't Understand?

Everyone is impacted by something that blocks the path to achieving a goal. These blockades shouldn't be thought of as only belonging to poor performers. It's no surprise that most externally motivated people will disagree with this. They use these impediments as their own personal excuses to justify their inability to accomplish the desired outcome. They view these things as happening only to them and not to those who achieved a successful outcome. Whatever is keeping them from attaining success becomes their personal excuse for failure. Externally motivated people not only believe this kind of thinking is okay and correct, they expect others to believe it too. When others disagree, it is common to hear these people say, "Well, you just don't understand the situation I am in" or, "You really don't know the problems I have. I simply don't have a lot of choices." They do not comprehend how internally motivated people think because they've never learned to think that way.

Along the way, externally motivated people didn't learn everything they needed to know about adversity. They learned something different than the high performers learned. They learned to be stopped by obstacles because they missed the lessons that would have convinced them that obstacles can be conquered. They never became aware of the fact that that their attitude toward obstacles is what determines their response to obstacles. They never learned to persevere and seek solutions. Instead, they learned it's okay to quit trying as long as you have an excuse for why. They grew up believing that achievement occurs only when nothing gets in the way. Low performers often believe it's others who don't understand, when in reality, it's the low performers who don't.

On-Again, Off-Again Motivation

Individuals who are externally motivated do have spurts of motivation because of the coming and going of obstacles, setbacks, disappointments, failures, curveballs, good days and bad days, and so on. Their self-motivation is on when things are humming along fine and off when they aren't. That's when they need external motivators to keep them engaged. Incentives, rewards, recognition, coaching, counseling, disciplinary action, and other common employee engagement tactics are no more than external motivators designed to "push start" an unmotivated employee. The problem is, when the fire from these external motivators go out, any beneficial effect they might have had ceases. Employees who need a push start will always accomplish less than they are capable of.

On-again, off-again motivation wreaks havoc on results. The only motivation that has maximum sustaining power is the kind where the fire to achieve burns within. Those who are internally motivated and have a passion for their work have an abundant source of self-motivation. These people will always achieve more than those who rely on an external source to motivate them. The greater the ability to put oneself into motion, the greater the accomplishments will be.

Wrapping Up Part I

Assessing motivation often goes astray when a candidate provides an example of being motivated to an inadequately trained interviewer who jumps to the conclusion that the candidate is self-motivated. In reality, every candidate can talk about a time they were motivated or took action, even if they are a poor performer. Individual examples of behavior cannot and do not quantify motivation. They neither provide the interviewer with the level of insight necessary to distinguish between spurts of motivation and sustained motivation, nor will they reveal whether the candidate had to be pushed to take the action or was self-motivated to take action. Finally, isolated instances of motivation won't help predict how interested the candidate will be to do the job after they're hired. The way interviewers have been assessing motivation in the past has been misguided. If they ended up hiring a high performer, it had more to do with good luck than anything else. All of that is about to change.

As we bring this chapter to a close, we've also completed Part I of the book. You should have a new and improved understanding about motivation and what makes high performers tick. You should have a solid understanding of the process of achievement and where it breaks down. Most of all, you should know exactly how high performers achieve better results while others don't. This is the foundation that everything is built on in Part II. Without the foundation, what comes next won't make sense. As we step into Part II, "Identifying High Performers," we will apply what we've learned so far to the interview process. We will address effective techniques for gathering quality candidate information as well as what information to gather, what questions to ask, and how to assess the answers candidates give. This wraps up Part I.

Notes

1. Simon Sinek, *Start with Why: How Great Leaders Inspire Everyone to Take Action* (New York: Portfolio/Penguin, 2009): 134.

2. Mark Abadi, "Eagles Quarterback Nick Foles' Super Bowl Victory Speech Has an Important Lesson about Failure," *Business Insider*, February 8, 2018 http://www.businessinsider.com/nick-foles-super-bowl-speech-failure-2018-2.

Part II

Identifying High Performers

Chapter 6

How to Get Your Candidates Talking

Interviewing effectiveness can be deceiving because even weak interviewers have some hiring successes, and even the best interviewers have hired an employee they wished they hadn't. There are many who make their job much more difficult than it has to be, however, by regularly hiring employees who perform below standards, quit too soon, or fail in some other way. Making good hiring decisions is not something that just happens. Hiring well is something all interviewers can and should learn to do. In this chapter, our next step will be to focus on specific pointers that address how to gather candidate information effectively. This includes creating the right environment and using techniques that encourage candidates to tell you more and to tell you things they may not otherwise disclose. You only have two choices: you can find out about the candidate before you hire, or you can wait until after they're hired. You choose.

I once worked with a director of training who had a reputation for hiring assistants who would stay for only three to four months. The company, as a whole, had relatively low turnover. Like so many, this director of training did not want to believe that her hiring decisions had anything to do with bad hires or her department's high turnover. Oftentimes, interviewers want to attribute turnover to something outside of their control, such as the work pace, the pay scale, or even the candidate—all of which are issues that can be effectively addressed during an interview. I realize it can feel uncomfortable to admit that we have an area with room for improvement.

If you never open yourself up to grow, however, your interviewing skill will never improve, and you will continue to make needless hiring mistakes.

Understanding the Interview Relationship

Learning how to get candidates to open up and speak freely is crucial for information gathering, and ultimately, hiring success. As interviewers, we must learn how to create the optimal interviewing environment, one that encourages dialogue. There are specific dos and don'ts that will help us do this. Before we can learn specific techniques however, we must understand the interaction that occurs between interviewers and job candidates.

There's a tacit relationship that automatically occurs and it is about control over the job offer. Initially, interviewers have control because it's the interviewer's prerogative to determine who gets hired and who doesn't. Even if a candidate doesn't really want the job, *all candidates, without exception, want the job offer.* No candidate wants to be rejected. This forces candidates into the role of saying what they need to say to get the offer. They sell themselves by accentuating their positives, by minimizing their negatives, and by providing the "right" answers to interview questions. Only at the point that candidates receive a job offer do they gain the control. Then they have the power to say yes or no and to negotiate a higher salary. This relationship of control is called the *interview relationship* and it automatically exists between every interviewer and candidate 100 percent of the time. It also makes the task of gathering quality candidate information a bit more challenging.

When it comes to gathering candidate information, interviewers typically have a fixed or limited amount of time to collect all the information they need. Untrained interviewers often don't make good use of their interviewing time. Instead of encouraging open dialogue, they stifle it. They often ask ineffective interview questions.

If they show the wrong type of response, a candidate can clam up or change their story to one that earns a better response from the interviewer. If interviewers aren't careful, they can negatively affect the information gathering process, causing them to skew their view of a candidate.

Relaxing Defenses

Most candidates come to the interview somewhat nervous or apprehensive, and with their guard up. The more at ease they feel while speaking with the interviewer, the more the information will flow. Relaxed candidates talk more freely while uptight ones remain guarded. It's when candidates feel more relaxed that closely held information they might be protecting tends to slip out.

I remember many years ago in Colorado Springs I interviewed a candidate for a retail management position. A district manager was with me, but I was asking most of the questions. The candidate was currently employed and had been at this job for a little less than two years. In response to one of my questions, he stated his last performance evaluation was about two months ago. He continued to answer the question by adding that one of things he needed to work on before his next evaluation in thirty days was to improve labor costs. After we finished, and the candidate left, the district manager immediately turned to me and said, "How did you get him to tell you that?" As the reader, did you catch the information the candidate let slip out? The district manager certainly did, and so did I. The candidate was on a ninety-day performance probation. He was job hunting before he got fired. Did I know about this information when the candidate walked in the door and did I then coax it out of him? Absolutely not. You never know who has negative information they are trying to hide and who doesn't. As an interviewer, you must become a master at creating the right environment, so that candidates will let their guard down and feel comfortable sharing information about themselves.

"So what if the candidate is nervous—that's their issue, right?" Many interviewers believe that candidates should adapt to them, not the other way around. After all, it's the interviewer who is in charge. Some interviewers will jump to the conclusion that a nervous candidate couldn't possibly be a high performer. That's simply not true. As the interviewer, it's to your advantage to make the adjustment. A relaxed feeling on the part of the candidate may not occur automatically but you can foster one and sustain it just by managing the interview environment. Doing this only requires two simple steps, and it's two steps that should become a part of every interview process.

Step 1: Relax the Candidate

The way the interview begins can have a dramatic effect on information gathering and on the entire interview. The importance of starting the interview off right isn't emphasized enough. Giving nervous candidates extra time to relax before jumping into your interview questions takes conscious effort, but it's a habit that's well worth the effort. Setting the stage for information to flow freely is not difficult to do. Interviewers who assign too little importance to this step will reduce their bounty.

Here's how it works: A candidate erects a wall to keep some information from escaping, just as if they were preparing for an interrogation. It's possible for this wall to stay up during the entire interview. This defensive shield begins to lower when there are no signs or reasons for apprehension. It is lowered even more when feelings of congeniality and rapport develop.

So, how long does it take to relax a candidate? It can take just a few minutes, or in some cases it may take ten minutes or more. It varies because every person is different. Each candidate comes to the interview with a different comfort level. Don't make the mistake of assuming that the most confident one will necessarily do the best job. High performers can feel just as nervous as anyone else. Some candidates are comfortable during an interview simply because they've had a lot of practice interviewing. This has no bearing on job performance. The goal is to hire the candidate who will do the best job, not the one who just interviews the best.

I'm also not a proponent of using body language to predict future job performance. A long time ago when I owned and operated my own recruiting agency, a sales manager once told me he would never hire anyone who had a wimpy handshake. From that point forward, I coached every candidate I sent to that sales manager on how to give a firm handshake. My point is body language can be taught and consciously controlled during an interview in order to project a false impression to the interviewer. Furthermore, I don't believe there is certain body language or other physical clues that are exclusive to high performers or low performers.

That being said, interviewers can use body language as a good indicator to determine a candidate has relaxed and settled in enough for the interview to proceed. Tense or nervous people often look like they have a rod in their spine, resulting in an upright and rigid appearance. This causes their shoulders to be in more of an upward position. As they begin to relax, the spine curves and the shoulders slowly drop into a more relaxed, natural position. They become less rigid and sit in a more casual and comfortable manner in their chair. Hands are another clue. When a candidate's hands are tightly clenched together or the candidate is fidgeting, you can assume there's some level of tension and nervousness. When the candidate first sits down, mentally note their body language and stiffness. Everyone has a different comfort level while being interviewed. We're not looking for a specific level of relaxation that everyone achieves, rather we're looking for signs of *change*. That change may not be dramatic. Some people will walk in the door more relaxed than others will ever become, and that's okay. This is nothing more than a visual clue to help the interviewer know when to move deeper into the interviewing process. This is by no means is an indicator of who should be hired and who shouldn't. Look for these clues and adjust *your* approach as warranted. Start out with small talk. Remember, some candidates take longer to warm up than others do. A college student or someone who has not interviewed in a long time may feel more apprehensive at first. Adjust the warm-up time on the front end of the interview until you notice that your candidate begins to relax. Regardless of how long this takes, it's crucial to see it through. The payoff can be significant, and that's why you are doing it.

Here are some tips for relaxing the candidate and maximizing the flow of information:

» Begin the interview with good eye contact and a genuine smile. Smiles work wonders to break the ice and befriend a person.

» Start off by easing into the interview gradually. Spend several minutes making small talk about the weather, traffic, getting to the interview site, and so on. Avoid anything political or controversial.

» Offer the candidate a beverage if possible.

» Interview in a distraction-free environment. Turn off any mobile devices, and forward the phone in the room to voicemail. Leave instructions not to be interrupted. Interruptions can make the candidate feel less important.

» Explain the interview format, which is that you will be reading questions and taking notes.

» Ask the candidate to hold any questions until the end of the interview. Explain that you will be happy to answer any questions they have at that time.

During that final question-and-answer session where they are asking you questions, you'll want to be prepared to provide a realistic timeline for when a decision will be made on filling the job and any next steps (the sooner the better in a tight labor market).

Do what it takes to encourage the best flow of information. You may feel that you don't have time to coddle a nervous candidate, but what you *really* don't have time for is a bad hire. The candidate who isn't adept at interviewing may still be a high performer. What we're looking for has nothing to do with the candidate's interviewing acumen but rather with their ability and motivation to perform after they're hired. Personally, I want all the information that I can obtain to make my decision—*especially the information the candidate feels a need to guard.* It's vital that you allocate sufficient time and attention to this initial step in the interview process.

Step 2: Show No Negative Judgment
Once you've established a relaxed environment, it's important to keep it. This next step is one of the most powerful and effective interviewing techniques there is. It can level the playing field when dealing with interview-savvy candidates and even give interviewers the advantage.

Have you noticed how divisive politics can be? Take President Trump for example. People either love him or hate him. If you're a Trump supporter or a nonsupporter, when you cross paths with a like-minded individual, the conversation flows effortlessly on that topic. Each person agrees with and reinforces the points the other person made and then adds their own. It's a safe environment to share your opinion.

I was recently in the company of a client who had a viewpoint that was in opposition to mine on this particular topic, but I was careful not to let on. I respected her right to think differently. The more I sought to understand her point of view without showing negative judgment or contrary belief, the more she opened up and shared her perspective. As a result, the conversation was enjoyable rather than constrained and tense. In this situation, I had nothing to gain by inserting my point of view. This strategy should be applied to the interview process as well.

Any hint of negative judgment or reaction of disapproval during an interview has quite a bit of destructive power. It damages trust, instantly causes the candidate's guard to go up, and undermines your interviewing ability. All of this serves to impede the flow of vital information that would otherwise be accessible to you.

As an interviewer, it is not as easy as you may think it is to conceal your reactions. Most interviewers feel confident in their ability to camouflage their negative reactions, when in fact they shouldn't be. While you're reading the candidate, and getting a feel for who they are, the candidate is doing the same thing with you. While you are asking your interview questions, writing your notes, and thinking follow-up questions, your candidate has nothing better to do than watch you, pick up signals, and try to figure you out.

Think about how easy it is to read the reaction of another person. Oftentimes it's easy to pick up on what another person is thinking or feeling even if they don't want you to. All you have to do is look for some outward physical clues. Both negative and positive responses have their own distinctive tone of voice, facial gestures, and even body language. A grin shows approval while a frown or folded arms send a very different message. The tone of a person's voice and even their eyes often provide unmistakable clues. Reactions are very telling. As the interviewer, it's difficult to be aware of all the messages you constantly communicate to the candidate with your own body language. Just because we don't speak doesn't mean that someone, in this case the candidate, can't pick up on what we are thinking. People can hone in on the reaction of others—especially when they're focused on it, and that's exactly what the candidate is doing. Can you recall a time when a friend asked you about an interview that you went on? Were you able to pick up some signs about how well you thought it went? What exactly were you picking up on that gave you this impression? If it wasn't something the interviewer actually said, then what was it? This is the same thing that your candidates are picking up from you, so remembering your experiences on the other side of the process will help.

After a candidate responds to one of your interview questions, they are looking at you for your reaction. Are you pleased or showing disapproval? When candidates pick up an indication that their answer was good, they feel good. There's a sense of rapport. This sends the message that the interviewer and the candidate are clicking and it's a safe place to share personal information. This higher level of trust further encourages candidates to relax and talk openly. Gradually they let their guard down even more. On one particular occasion, a candidate asked if she could be honest with me. I smiled and said, "Of course." She proceeded to tell me how unfair she thought it was that she didn't get promoted on her last job. She continued on by sharing that her boss often bragged about not being honest on her tax returns. She finished the story by telling me that she made an anonymous call to the IRS and it wasn't long before her boss was complaining about being audited. It's amazing what people will share with you during a job interview when they don't feel like they are being negatively judged.

If candidates pick up any indication that their answer wasn't what you wanted to hear, then a completely different reaction takes place. Remember that the candidate's goal is to get the job offer, which means they are forced into a role of trying to give good answers. Have you ever had a candidate amend, change, or correct something they said? As interviewers, we all have. The only reason this happens is because the candidate picked up on some hint of negative judgment. You may not realize that you were outwardly broadcasting your disapproval, but you did, and the candidate intercepted it. When this happens, it doesn't help any interviewer. There is absolutely nothing to gained by exhibiting a negative or disapproving response.

Now, I don't want you to get confused. I'm not asking you to master a poker face. It is not enough to just conceal a negative judgment; you must go a step further. *The secret is to get into the habit of displaying an agreeing or empathetic response to the candidate's answers.* It can be subtle. A simple smile and positive nod will generally work. A sympathetic or warm tone of voice works extremely well. You have to come across as sincere and believable, without appearing pretentious. This becomes more difficult to do on those occasions when a candidate discloses information that you happen to find disconcerting. Absolutely *any* negative reaction at that moment will cause your candidate to shut you out just when you want him to tell you more. You especially don't want the candidate to backpedal here. You want them to feel comfortable enough with you to continue to speak openly and tell you more. Otherwise, they will hold back information that might help you avoid making a serious hiring mistake. Disapproval is not conducive to a candidate receiving a job offer. You have the right to negatively judge, *you just can't show any of it*. Keep it to yourself—it doesn't benefit you!

When teaching an interviewer training workshop, sometimes I'll conduct a skill-building exercise where attendees get to see exactly how candidates interpret an interviewer's responses. Then we practice coming up with better ones. It sounds simple, but it's not as easy it seems. The attendees are the interviewers, and I play the candidate. I give them an interviewing scenario where they just asked me why I want to leave my current job. Then I disclose a shocking tidbit—that I'm about to go ballistic if my current boss doesn't quit picking on me. I realize this is an extreme scenario, but it works well to make a point. Attendees are challenged to respond to me in a way that will persuade me to disclose more information. My guard must remain down, or they won't get more details from me. For those who've attended a workshop where I've used this exercise, you already know exactly what I'm talking about. We usually have to go through half a dozen or more people before someone responds in a way that actually persuades me (the candidate) to spill the beans. Here's the kicker: I'm not the one who's judging the responses. Everyone else in the class is, which reveals how easy it is for candidates to read interviewers. Responses that may seem perfect to obtain more information are viewed as suspect in the eyes of the candidate. You'd be surprised how even a well-meaning, neutral response with no sign of negative judgment can still come across as being somewhat judgmental, causing candidates to be leery and raise their guard.

This point is so important it's not only explained in MBI workshops, but a visual prop is used to further emphasize the point.

Remember when I said a simple smile and positive nod works well? The prop that is used is a bobblehead with a giant smile. When you touch the head the smiling face bobs up and down. That's the visual image interviewers need to have in their head regarding how they should react to every candidate answer no matter what they say. Certified MBI Trainers even get this prop to share it in the classes that they teach. Go ahead—practice smiling and nodding now.

What I want you to realize is that interviewers need to go the extra mile here. The kind of conversation that occurs when two people connect is not something that either has to happen naturally or not at all: you can help it along. As the interviewer, you can project a facade that facilitates a personal connection and encourages candidates to disarm. By doing this, we're fostering an environment that has the feel of total acceptance and complete approval to all the candidate's answers. For some interviewers, this feels uncomfortable and quite unnatural, while for others it's easy. You are not changing how you feel, you're simply keeping your own feelings private while encouraging the candidate to express theirs. Don't worry if your true feelings differ; that's perfectly okay. There is no rule that states interviewers must outwardly express their own viewpoint to the candidate. Furthermore, *there is absolutely nothing wrong with your candidate feeling good about their interview and leaving with their self-esteem intact*, even if they didn't make a good impression. After all, their mission was to show you their best side. Your mission is to identify and hire only the best. It's about playing the interviewing game to win, and winning means hiring high performers!

Here are some tips for showing no negative judgment:

» If the candidate talks about their frustration with a prior work situation, you should appear to be empathetic, and most importantly, be on their side.

» Smile to encourage the candidate to tell you more without fear of reprisal.

> » Let the candidate believe you know exactly how they feel—"Yeah, I can understand. Tell me more."
> » Come across as if you can relate to the candidate's situation. This will help to establish trust and make the candidate feel as if they can tell you anything.
> » Be especially careful not to appear to be critical. We've already emphasized how detrimental that can be.

These are highly effective techniques for gathering information. This may seem like a game that you don't want to play, but candidates are becoming *very* interview savvy. There is a flood of information, all readily accessible from the candidate's smartphone, designed to help them ace the interview. Interviewers deserve the same opportunity. When it comes to information gathering, getting into the habit of making all candidates feel at ease benefits *you* the most. It will ensure that the interviewer retains the upper hand, regardless of how savvy the candidate may be. We need candidates to feel that they can confide in us. That's the goal, and have no doubt—it's possible!

Whose Side Are You On?

As the leading expert on interviewing and hiring, I can't tell you how frequently I'm asked whether it's okay to offer advice to candidates about how they should answer interview questions. Yes, some interviewers actually coach job candidates on how to answer their interview questions *while the interview is taking place*. Sometimes, if the candidate doesn't answer a question well, the interviewer will keep prodding and encouraging them for a better answer. What these interviewers don't realize is, *a bad answer is still an answer.* The problem with hiring isn't that we have too many employees who exceed our expectations; if that were the case, we wouldn't have a problem. The opposite is true. We have too many employees who are falling short of our expectations. The person who showed up for the job interview doesn't seem to be the same person who showed up for the job. What's happening is that interviewers are overrating some of their candidates. These highly rated candidates seem great to the interviewer, so of course they're hired. The problem is that when candidates are overrated, they will underperform... because they are overrated.

Many interviewers make the mistake of providing candidates with too much information up front about the job or the ideal candidate. This can actually backfire and filter the flow of information as candidates adjust their answers to better fit the job and match the interviewer's description of an ideal hire. Below is an example of asking an interview question in a way that clues in the candidate. The question is formed in such a way that it guides the candidate to the answer the interviewer most likely wants to hear.

» **Interviewer:** "As you know, you are here today interviewing for a cashier position within the theme park. Just to let you know, we provide a fifteen-minute break for every four-hour shift you work. Sometimes however, when the park is really busy and the lines are long, your break could be delayed or even bypassed. If that were to happen, how would you feel about that?"

Do you think someone who is a chronic complainer will actually speak up during the interview and voice their concern about missing breaks? Assuming they want the job, the odds of that happening are probably about the same as the odds printed on your lottery ticket. In fact, they may even talk about how "very tolerant" they would be with missed breaks because they "understand the nature of the business." If they are hired, though, their true colors would start to show, of course. During the interview, the answers they give won't reflect who they really are or how they behave, because they give what is immediately obvious to them as the right answer. They may not be high performers, but they know a gift when they see one.

Sometimes extra assistance is offered only to candidates who are favored rather than to every candidate. That kind of practice is of no benefit to the interviewer because it contributes to embellishment, distorts information, and compromises candidate comparisons. Every candidate should be given the opportunity to stand equally on their own merits, not only for the sake of gathering accurate information, but also to ensure fairness and integrity. No guidance, accidentally or intentionally, should be provided. Remember this: *offering any additional information about the job prior to the interview benefits only the candidate, not the interviewer.* If it is the interviewer's intent to explain or sell the job, there are better ways to do this that won't have a negative impact on the selection process. Simply save this information till the end of the interviewing process.

> *Interviewers should never do the majority of the talking during an interview.*

One of the most challenging hiring scenarios I see frequently is when sales managers interview sales candidates. It's not uncommon for sales managers who lack the proper interviewer training to spend too much time during the interview talking up the job. *Interviewers should never do the majority of the talking during an interview.* When the interviewer is talking, the candidate is not. That means candidate information isn't being gathered. Ultimately, that will negatively affect the hiring decision, which depends heavily on collecting as much quality information as possible about every candidate.

This scenario gets worse. On the other side of the desk you have candidates who are selling themselves because they're interviewing for a sales job. You have a whole lot of selling going on, on both sides. Furthermore, many sales managers incorrectly believe that any candidate who is extroverted will be a good salesperson. Being outgoing is not an indicator of how a person will respond when given a lofty sales quota, when they need to close sales that involve stiff competition, or when they aren't able to offer the lowest price. Hiring for sales is mission-critical because these employees are the organization's revenue generators. Wise sales managers (and CEOs) understand that spending money on the right interviewer training has a profound return on the investment.

Asking Questions That Have Obvious Right Answers

It's not hard to imagine how the interview relationship would affect how a candidate answers the following questions:

» **Question 1:** Are you self-motivated?
» **Candidate's Answer:** Absolutely yes!

» **Question 2:** Do you think initiative is important?
» **Candidate's Answer:** Without a doubt!

» **Question 3:** On a scale of one to ten, how much effort do you put into your work?
» **Candidate's Answer:** Eleven. I always go the extra mile!

Many interviewers ask questions without first thinking about how the interview relationship might affect the answer candidates give. If there is an obvious right answer, you can be fairly certain that's the one candidates are going to provide. After all, how would you answer those questions if you were the candidate? Do you really think a candidate will admit to not being self-motivated during a job interview? Will any candidate say they are below a six or seven on the effort scale? If fact, most will rate themselves a ten, or even higher. How about saying that initiative is not important? And even if you ask every candidate to provide an example of a time they started something, took initiative, or demonstrated self-motivation, everyone can share at least one example. That's because there is no such thing as zero motivation. Even poor performers have one example, and I'm betting that's the one they're going to share with you. You get the point.

When it comes to asking interview questions, sometimes taking a more indirect approach yields better results because the right and wrong answers are less obvious. If candidates aren't high performers, they're pretending to be, because every candidate is a high performer in their own mind. Your interview process needs to distinguish between who really is one and who isn't. That's what MBI does.

R-E-S-P-E-C-T

Always, always treat every candidate with the utmost respect. Even if you don't hire someone, that person could be a current or future customer or could refer other candidates to you! I remember hearing stories about a large retail organization who would take management candidates through their hiring process, first interviews, second interviews, and more, and then stop communicating with them. No job offers, but also no thanks-but-no-thanks letters or emails and no return phone calls either. Eventually the candidates figured out the company was no longer interested in pursuing employment opportunities with them. Some people told me that they were so put off by how they were treated that they would never shop at that retailer again. I don't know if there is any connection, but that particular organization went out of business several years later.

My point is that you always want to treat job candidates just as you like to be treated—with dignity and respect. It's not only something you do during the information-gathering process, it's something you do through the entire process. If you tell a candidate that you're going to make your hiring decision and notify them by a certain date, do it! If things come up and you don't have a decision by that date, you still need to let them know the date has been pushed back. Job offers are a big deal. A person's life revolves around their job and their paycheck. Candidates get frustrated, justifiably so, when employers don't keep their word. I can't tell you how many times I've heard people say, "Even if they offer me a job, I'm not going to accept it. If they can't keep their word before I'm hired, they're probably not going to afterward either."

All of the interviewing techniques recommended in this chapter are highly effective. As simple as they are, they're not known to many interviewers. Sadly, it's fairly common for anyone in management who sits behind a desk and asks a few questions to be dubbed "interviewer." These managers interview candidates and make hiring decisions, and come to believe that they've become experts at interviewing and hiring by virtue of experience alone. The truth is that it doesn't work that way.

The simple fact is that organizations that don't make the investment to train hiring managers to be effective interviewers are gradually falling behind those who do. In the long run, he who hires poorly shall perish.

Now that we've learned how to get the candidates talking, it's time to build upon the information-gathering foundation and learn exactly what interview questions we need to ask.

Chapter 7

MBI Interview Questions

Every chapter in this book is essential. This chapter, however, is an especially important chapter. If you don't fully grasp the concepts presented in this one and follow them implicitly—I'll be blunt—you will fail at MBI.

As mentioned in Chapter 1, "The State of Hiring," behavior-based interviewing is the Wild West of interviewing because other than asking candidates for behavior examples, almost anything else goes. That's a problem when it comes to gathering information and being able to correctly distinguish high performers from the general population of candidates. MBI closes the holes and fills the gaps that behavior-based interviewing leaves unresolved. That means MBI imposes structure and has some specific rules that *must* be followed. It's not complicated or difficult to use. MBI works, and works well—but only if you understand it and use it properly.

As we've already established, all high performers have three things in common: *skill, attitude,* and *passion.* It's this trio that enables the high performer to achieve superior results. So, naturally, in order to identify high performers, skill, attitude, and passion all need to be assessed. If you have interviewing and hiring experience, it's likely that you've only been assessing one of these three ingredients: skill. I know what you're thinking: MBI is going to require three times as much time because of these extra assessments, right? No, no, and no! MBI doesn't take *any* additional interviewing time. Here's a quick overview of how it works:

» In MBI, skill questions double as locus of control questions. That means skill questions now gather two types of information about the candidate. Interviewers can harvest locus of control information without the need to add any additional interview questions.

» Gathering information about a candidate's passion entails asking five simple prewritten Career Fit questions that take no more five to ten minutes of interviewing time in total.

» Except for relaxing the candidate, reviewing work history and education, and wrapping up the interview, that's the entire MBI process.

It's structured but simple. It's about becoming lean, mean interviewing machines! Alright, maybe not *mean*. All we're really doing is teaching you how to become a highly effective interviewer who knows exactly what candidate information to go after and how to get it.

Introduction to MBI Questions

Since Career Fit questions are prewritten, the bulk of our focus is going to be on how to write questions that will assess a candidate's skill and locus of control. These questions are skill-specific. Skills can be broken into three types: *technical*, *soft*, and *core*.

Technical skills typically involve the skill, knowledge, and ability required to perform jobs such as math, science, technology, and even language. These questions tend to have a single, clear-cut correct answer. For example: the right answer for 1 + 1 is always and only 2.

Soft skills include skills such as customer service, teamwork, and sales. They tend to involve people and communication. Right answers are more subjective and what the right answer is often varies between people, meaning two people can hear the same answer but score it differently.

Core competencies can be either technical or soft skills, but more often than not they are soft skills. These are simply skills required for all jobs. Punctuality, commitment to excellence, and ethics are examples of skills an organization might deem that everyone should have.

How to Structure O-SAE Questions

MBI skill-assessment questions are formed using the acronym O-SAE. It's called the "Oh-Say" method, as in, "Oh, say, can you see if you have a high performer?" In addition, three simple rules must always be followed. These rules ensure the questions are formatted and phrased properly so that they actually gather the intended information. Without these rules, interviewers often end up asking ineffective interview questions that low performers can easily answer well. How do we expect to be able to identify high performers when the questions we're asking won't produce answers that will enable us to do so? The answer is that we can't, at least not with any degree of consistency.

In the O-SAE method, each skill-assessment question has three parts, which are more like three separate questions. *O-S* represents the first question, *A* represents the second question, and *E* represents the third question. Below are the words that each letter represents::

- » **O-S** = Obstacle-Situation
- » **A** = Actions taken
- » **E** = End results

The A and E questions are prewritten and never have to change. All of the effort involved in writing O-SAE questions falls into constructing the second half of the O-S question, the first half also being prewritten. The O-S questions always start out "Tell me about a specific time when..." The second half must be written by you.

Let me provide some insight. *The key to determining locus of control is to learn how a person responds to adversity.* Plugging a real-life, on-the-job obstacle into your interview questions, specifically into the O-S part, will be what ultimately reveals a candidate's locus of control. Remember, in the process of achievement, the obstacle creates the fork in the road where high performers take one path and low performers take a different route. To expose which path a person takes in the face of challenge, an obstacle of some kind is mandatory in every O-S question. Otherwise, we cannot and will not gather the locus of control information that is always there and readily available. Locus of control is a powerhouse predictor of future performance. It would be detrimental to miss it.

Let's also talk about the A and E questions so that you have the fundamentals of the O-SAE method before we dive deeper into the O-S question. Following the first question comes a request for any action the candidate took (in response to the obstacle), which is followed up with the last question requesting the outcome. For example, the A question simply prompts, "Tell me about the actions you took," and the E question is "What were the end results?" You do not need to customize either of these questions, *and I caution you not to*. However, you do have a little wiggle room in the A and E questions. For instance, for the action-taken question you can also say, "So, what did you do?" or "What steps did you take?" or "How did you handle it?" or a similar variation. You can do the same thing with the end-result question. You could also say, "So, what happened?" or "What was the outcome?" or "How did it turn out?" It's very important that you understand that you cannot go beyond the boundaries I've set forth without compromising the effectiveness of your interview questions.

The Three Rules

You must know the three rules in order to write the second half of your O-S questions. I'm going to show you all three of the rules first, and discuss them second:

Rule 1: One Obstacle—Include only one obstacle per question.

Rule 2: Open Outcome—Don't ask for a successful or a failed outcome. Leave it open.

Rule 3: Specific—Ask for the *specific* details. (This is the interviewer's power word!)

Rule one requires that you always include one and only one obstacle in each and every O-S question. If you have more than one obstacle, create a second question. It's perfectly fine to ask multiple questions pertaining to the same skill.

> *Never* assume your candidate took action or achieved a good outcome.

Rule two requires that you always keep the outcome open and *never ask for examples of success or failure*. Sometimes interviewers also try to slip "success" into the A question by asking what actions the candidate took to meet the deadline, achieve the goal, satisfy the customer, or similar. *Never* assume your candidate took action or achieved a good outcome. Don't help them out. That's going to lead them to give you a good answer. Gathering information related to a result is the sole purpose of the E question. By following this guideline, we are allowing the candidate to pick their own stories to share. Sometimes they will surprise you by responding with an unexpected or even shocking outcome. I once interviewed a candidate in Stone Mountain, Georgia, (a suburb of Atlanta) for a restaurant management position. I asked an O-SAE question about dealing with an irate customer. He actually answered the O-S and A portions well, but I didn't see his E answer coming. He gave me specific details of a situation involving a yelling, disgruntled customer and talked about how he pulled the customer to the side, listened, apologized, and asked what he could do to make things right. Then I asked, "What were the end results?" He answered by saying he called the cops on the customer and told him to never come back. He said he just got tired listening to him. I smiled and nodded as if I could relate and displayed no hint of negative judgment. I also didn't hire this guy. It's in the interviewer's best interest to always leave the outcome open because you can't make assumptions about the outcome. Had I asked for a success story, I seriously doubt that he would have considered sharing that story. But that was the story I needed to hear to avoid a potential hiring mistake!

Rule three states that the word "specific" must *always* be used in the O-S question. That means 100 percent of the time. Here's why: *The only person who can talk about their specific problem-solving efforts and provide all the underlying detail about the actions they took is someone who actually did the work.*

Even if the candidate can provide these specifics, if you don't ask outright, there's no guarantee they will volunteer to share the details with you. You have to ask because otherwise you won't know who has them and who doesn't. It also means that you won't be able to accurately distinguish between the high performer and the low performer. That's why "specific" is the interviewer's power word. Just as those who actually went into problem-solving mode can speak specifically about the experience, those who didn't go into problem-solving mode and didn't try very hard to overcome the obstacle cannot talk about the specific details of the action they took, because those details simply don't exist. The best these people can do is explain why they didn't do the work, or offer up a generic, nonspecific answer they believe sounds reasonable. It's a night–and-day difference compared to the answer an authentic high performer will provide. It stands out like a sore thumb. This distinction is plain to see as long as the questions are phrased correctly.

Here's one more pointer: Until you get into the habit of saying, "Tell me about a *specific* time when... " you might find that you are leaving out the word "specific." Or maybe you say it but your candidate is nervous and misses it. You are allowed to nudge your candidate once—and only once—per skill question if they give you a generic answer. I'm not talking about going as far as coaching or guiding them to a right answer; just make sure you said it and they heard it. You can reiterate it by saying, "Do you have a specific example?" If they have one, they'll share one. If they don't, they will do nothing more than repackage what they just said, in which case simply smile and nod. You have your answer.

How to Add an Obstacle

Now that you have the three rules, we can start applying them to writing O-S questions.

Most of our focus is going to be placed on how to add an obstacle into your questions. Getting this step right is imperative for correctly assessing motivation. Including an obstacle in a question is achieved by adding one or two descriptive words—usually adjectives—that characterize a situation as challenging or difficult. Time or money aren't problems when we have plenty of them. They become problems, or obstacles, when we don't have enough. Words like *insufficient, inadequate, not enough*, or *lacked* can all be used as obstacles (but only one at a time). Below are two examples:

» Tell me about a specific time when you *lacked* the time necessary to achieve a goal.
» Tell me about a specific time when you were asked to achieve goals with an *insufficient* budget.

There are a lot of obstacle word options. You could have an *uncooperative, annoying*, or *unprepared* teammate. How about having to communicate a *tough, vague*, or *unwelcome* policy change? You pick the adjective that best applies to your specific workplace.

Questions that specifically ask for a success story, such as, "Tell me about a specific time you went above and beyond to satisfy a customer," can easily cause interviewers to overrate candidates. It turns a one-to-five skill-scoring scale into more of a three-to-five scale. When candidates share a success story (because you asked for a time they "went above and beyond"), it eliminates the need for the lower-end scores. That question, and many others like it, will reap only answers that have happy endings, resulting in scores of four or five. That wouldn't be a problem if everyone deserved the high customer service rating and performed at that level after they were hired. But that's simply not the case. We have a problem of epidemic proportion with poor customer service. As customers, it's not uncommon to receive average service, which qualifies as a three or worse on our scale. Receiving excellent or even above-average customer service is the exception, not the norm. Those top-tier scores that are being gratuitously doled out for happily ending answers aren't representative of the real world.

So, let's see if MBI fixes this issue. By adding an obstacle into your interview questions, and following the other rules, can we widen the range of possible responses? For example, if I say to the candidate, "Tell me about a specific time when you dealt with an irate customer," could I get average answers where the candidate satisfied the customer but did nothing more? Sure. Is it possible I could get an answer that the candidate not only satisfied the customer but went further? Again, yes. Is it also possible I could get an answer where the candidate insisted the customer was impossible to please or that there was nothing else they could do to resolve the problem? You get the idea. Unlike when I ask for a success story, I can now get a full range of responses, including the kind that would deserve a score in the lower range.

Things Can Go Wrong

As interviewers, we need to become smart about the interview questions we ask. Learning how seems relatively simple, but it's also easy to get it wrong and make mistakes.

I recall one occasion when I personally taught a workshop for a client in Charlotte, North Carolina. As usual, I put a great deal of effort into explaining how to write O-S questions correctly. A few weeks after the workshop, the vice president of HR sent me the interview questions the class had written. There were four pages of questions with approximately fifteen questions per page. I didn't need to look at all sixty. Thirteen out of fifteen on the first page were ineffective questions. Some had no obstacle while others had two. There were some that requested a happy ending and others that asked about a time when the candidate failed. There were some that left out the word "specific" and others that had multiple issues. There was clearly a problem. I was a bit shocked, especially since I taught this class myself. When I spoke to the VP, I suggested that the hiring managers either had no interest in writing interview questions or they didn't take the time to do it right. He answered by saying he thought it was a little of both.

The reality is it can take more time to compose your questions than it takes to learn MBI. It's not something that can be delegated to HR to do for the hiring managers. It requires subject matter experts who know the ins and outs of the job, and especially the challenges. When interviewers go rogue with their questions, whether intentionally or by accident, MBI is not going to work as intended. It won't be possible to accurately assess a candidate's attitude or motivation. The bottom line is, don't assume that a properly trained interviewer who uses ineffective interview questions will still achieve maximum hiring results. *They won't.* I cannot stress this enough!

For organizations that want to hit the ground running using MBI immediately, Hire Authority offers a subscription-based MBI Interview Guide Generator with hundreds of ready-to-go O-SAE questions in seventy-five skill categories. At the time this book was written, the database of O-SAE questions contained more than 750 questions to choose from, with more being added regularly. Once an organization has subscribed, employees who have formal MBI training can use this tool to generate highly customizable MBI interview guides on demand, in minutes. If you would like to watch a short video of the MBI Interview Guide Generator in action, please visit www.hireauthority.com/membership.

Where to Begin

The good news is that when you compile a set of questions that work well, you can use them over and over again. Unless the job changes, the questions can be used for years. I've used the same set of questions to hire hospitality managers for two decades.

So how do you get started writing your questions? First you must identify the skills that are required to do the job: the technical, soft, and core competencies. Remember, O-SAE questions are skill-specific. Without a functional knowledge of the required job skills, you can't write O-SAE questions. Personally, I'm not a big fan of using job descriptions to compile a list of required skills. Depending how the job description is written—listing essential and nonessential job functions, ADA compliance, and so on—it can be challenging to derive what you need. I like to keep it simple.

At one point, I worked with a group of forty district managers to tackle this very task. We focused on one specific job and I asked for their input. Each time they gave me a skill I wrote it on a flip chart. We put together eleven skills and made sure we understood each one. Both time management and organizational skills were on the list. We needed to double check that we weren't describing the same skill two different ways. Did employees need to be organized so they managed their time well? It turns out that time management was about showing up for scheduled appointments with clients on time. Organizational skills were about being able to plan their day and their route efficiently because no one was going to do that for them.

Once the skills to do a particular job are properly identified, questions can be developed. I recommend writing a minimum of two O-SAE questions per skill. Once they're written, you'll need to test them, which means conducting a few interviews and actually asking them to some candidates. If you find that a question is awkward or never seems to elicit a useful response from the candidate, refine or replace it. Many organizations involve multiple interviewers and create multiple interview guides for the same position. These different guides are often called Interview Guide A and Interview Guide B.

Below is a sample list of skills for a basic management position:

» Profit and loss knowledge
» Controlling costs
» Building sales
» Customer service
» Hiring employees
» Terminating employees
» Training
» Coaching and counseling
» Communication skills

Let's use customer service. I'll share some of the questions in the database for that skill so that you'll have a few more examples of what good O-SAE questions look like:

» Tell me about a specific time when you encountered an overly demanding customer.
» Tell me about a specific time when you had to deal with an unhappy internal or external customer.
» Tell me about a specific time when a customer was rude to you.

Let me reiterate one point about building your skills list. We covered this in Chapter 4, but it's worth mentioning again: be careful how you think about unskilled candidates or about candidates who don't have exactly the skill set you're looking for. Have you ever complained that there aren't enough candidates to choose from because the pool of applicants has dried up? We have a tendency to think that high performers are only those candidates who have the perfect skills for our needs at the exact time we need them, and that if a candidate doesn't have those exact skills at the exact time, then they couldn't possibly be a high performer or a good hire. This thinking is inaccurate. It puts the emphasis on the timing of skill development rather than acknowledging that skill development is a lifelong process. All high performers had no skills at some point in the past but somehow ended up becoming high performers anyway. We don't want to use a list of required skills to exclude a highly motivated individual who will outperform the average employee when given the opportunity to acquire the skills. When we look at things from this perspective, perhaps our pool of applicants isn't as limited as we thought. If you have candidates with insufficient skills but the right attitude to achieve, it would be foolish to turn them away, assuming you are willing to provide training.

Locus of Control Questions for Entry-Level Jobs

One of the biggest benefits of MBI is the fact that it can be used effectively to hire entry-level employees. For entry-level positions, you may end up with a short list of required skills. If this is the case, you can always add in some generic locus of control interview questions. Basically, any question that involves an adversity of some kind is a locus of control question. Below are three examples:

» Tell me about a specific time when you struggled to do something that you did not know how to do.
» Tell me about a specific time when something (a project, a schedule, etc.) didn't go as you had wanted.
» Tell me about a specific time when you were in a new social situation and knew no one.

Get the idea? Everyone we could possibly interview, including teenagers who haven't graduated high school yet, have encountered obstacles. Just because candidates are light on skill or work experience doesn't mean they don't have any challenging experiences they can talk about. These questions are equally effective for candidates with a lot of experience as well, making them very versatile.

The Three Reasons to Always Phrase O-S Questions the Same Way

One of the most common questions I'm asked about MBI is whether O-S questions really need to be phrased, "Tell me about a specific time when..." every time. Can interviewers add some variety? The answer is yes to the first question and no to the second one. I'll give you the three reasons this is important.

Reason one is that consistently phrasing your questions a certain way will develop a good habit in you—for example, as discussed earlier, always remembering to use the word "specific."

Reason two is that when interviewers do something different and change how the question is formatted, more often than not they don't make the question better. Instead, they make it less effective without realizing that they have done so. Recently, an interviewer asked me if it was okay to rephrase the front half of the O-S this way: "Give me a meticulous example of a time..." *Meticulous?* There was no way that they could use "specific" and "meticulous" together, so "meticulous" was replacing the word "specific." In no way did this improve the interview question, and in fact it broke the third rule— to always use "specific," the interviewer's power word.

Reason three is that candidates don't mind. They have no problem with questions being presented to them in a consistent format. It has no ill effect. In fact, most people tend to view a structured process as being fairer and less biased.

Part of the reason MBI works so well is simply because *it is simple*. Making it more complex than it needs to be won't make it any better, and would actually be counterproductive. I'll share a story with you: There was once a large organization that spent tens of thousands of dollars developing a custom interview process for hiring managers. The company they hired to help them accomplish this came in and surveyed their current managers. After that, they created interview questions that were supposed to help the organization identify candidates who were more like the high performers they already had. In the end, what they were given was a thirteen-page interview guide that required days of training to learn. It also took as long as three hours per candidate just to conduct the interview. The interviewers were actually busy district managers who had a territory to cover and a multitude of other issues to deal with beyond hiring. For a time, the corporate office thought everyone was using this process, but the reality was that they weren't. The hiring managers took shortcuts and only asked certain questions to speed up the interview.

Just because an interview process takes a long time doesn't mean that it will be effective. Then there's this other minor detail: processes that aren't used are never effective. What is the moral? Something that is simple, but done right, can be highly effective. This describes MBI, and this is why the organization mentioned above switched to using MBI instead.

Follow-Up Questions

Before we move on to the Career Fit questions, I want to talk to you about asking follow-up questions. By now you should understand that your interview questions are created in advance of the interview. Follow-up questions, however, are not something you can anticipate. As candidates share answers, it's okay to ask additional questions to gain a better understanding of the whole story. Again, I'm not talking about coaching or leading the candidate into giving you a better response.

I once interviewed a guy in Warner Robbins, Georgia, a growing area just south of Macon. He spoke about his struggle with achieving a sales goal that he thought was unrealistic. He continued without sharing what the actual goal was. So, I asked him a follow-up question, "What was the goal?" He told me that it was to increase sales by 10 percent. That seemed steep. I knew the industry, and about a 6 percent increase over the year before is considered very good. I asked a few more follow-up questions. He managed a pizza delivery business and I came to find out that for years his was the only pizza place in town. As the area grew, sales increased easily by 12 percent annually. Then competition moved in and his sales increases began to decline. He shared with me that there was nothing he could do about it. Either customers came in or they didn't. The reality was, however, there were things he could do to build sales. My point here is you never want to move on until you understand the full story.

Interviewers should also pay close attention when they hear "we." Sometimes candidates will give an example from when they were part of a team effort and will use the word "we"—*we* did this, and *we* did that, and this is what *we* accomplished. There is nothing inherently wrong with this word. I recommend, however, that you ask the candidate some follow-up questions to find out exactly what role the candidate played and their level of participation. More than once I've discovered that I was likely interviewing the weak link on a team. They would have no problem taking credit for the team's results by using the word "we," but they seemed unable to share much detail about their contribution. You need to clarify and ask for more detail about exactly what the candidate did on the team or on the project.

It is up to the interviewer to be thorough. Make sure you ask appropriate follow-up questions as needed.

Capturing Passion

Now it's time to shift our focus on how we capture data about a candidate's passion. It's very different from gathering information on locus of control. Unlike locus of control questions, which are limitless in number, the questions that determine interest level are few, specific, and, best of all, already written for you.

Let's take a look at the big picture before we tackle the questions. Assessing passion is not a new concept. You will not be the first person to do this, not even close. Career counselors, mentors, teachers, professional career coaches, books, and tests have already been doing it for nearly a hundred years. In order to measure passion, interviewers must become, in essence, mini career counselors. It's mandatory.

The fundamental principle that career counselors use for assessment is to determine a person's likes, natural or developed abilities, and goals. Then they match the person with a compatible job. The object is to find a job that consists almost entirely of the kind of work the individual enjoys doing. The fewer dislikes, the better. This is exactly what Career Fit (see Chapter 4) is all about. It is a very simple concept: If you enjoy your work, you'll work harder and quite possibly stay in the job longer. If your job is not something you enjoy doing, then you'll lack interest, and you won't give it your all.

Do you remember from Chapter 4 why interest level is so important? It's the spark that starts everything. When a high level of interest is mixed with internal motivation, self-motivation results. Conversely, an insufficient interest level can cause motion to halt. Interests are simple to understand. As defined in Chapter 4, they are what a person likes to do, is good at doing, and wants to do more of—their likes, strengths, and goals. Interests are not those things we dislike such as anything that lacks appeal for us, those things we procrastinate doing, or tasks we find unpleasant, tedious, or boring. Everyone has likes and dislikes, and everyone's likes and dislikes are different. And that's okay.

Taking an Indirect Approach

The questions to assess a candidate's interests do not use the O-SAE method. More of an indirect approach is taken to gather this information. Asking the candidate directly what their perfect career choice is could get you a funny look, as if the answer is an obvious one.

Let's say for example that you are interviewing a candidate for a financial analyst job that you have open. In addition to the candidate having the skills you need, you want to make sure they are self-motivated to do this type of work. So, you ask the candidate straight on, "Is this a job that you will enjoy?" Can you figure out how most candidates will answer the question? If they have any interviewing sense at all, they'll say yes, that they love doing this type of work and it's exactly the job they're seeking. This is especially true if the person needs a job. As a headhunter, I've advised countless job seekers to say this. It's usually not beneficial for candidates to say anything other than that. Any other answer would be interview suicide. From my experience, there are many who have learned how to answer this question to please the interviewer. They tell interviewers exactly what they want to hear. And, as an interviewer, you can't tell the difference between a genuine answer and one that's being given solely because it's believed to be the right answer. Both responses sound credible. By using more of an indirect approach, we gather a better quality of candidate information and we bypass receiving only obvious, "right" answers. In essence, we're avoiding the unfavorable effects of the interview relationship that we discussed in Chapter 6.

Another good reason for using an indirect approach is that sometimes people truly don't know what kind of job they would enjoy doing the most. All they do know is that it's not what they're currently doing. If someone doesn't know, then asking them directly won't work well for assessing what motivates them. To understand the indirect approach, think about how a professional career counselor helps clients discover the best job match. When they start working with someone new, neither they nor their client knows the answer. However, that doesn't mean the career counselor can't discover it. Whether they use a test or ask questions verbally, the goal is to obtain specific information. Our goal is to get similar information by playing mini career counselor and asking a series of indirect questions. Using this method of inquiry, we can get a pretty good idea about what a good or bad job match will be, and it works equally well when candidates know what motivates them and when they don't know.

Now... the Career Fit Questions

The questions used to determine a candidate's passion will center around their likes, strengths, and goals. For the purpose of comparison, however, we also want to know what does *not* motivate that person. We're going to ask questions about the candidate's dislikes and weaknesses to gain that insight.

There are only five questions, and they pertain to likes and dislikes, strengths and weaknesses, and goals. They don't take very long to ask and are, for most candidates, painless to answer. There are also two very powerful locus of control questions woven in after the weakness and goals questions. In fact, these two questions are my all-time personal favorite locus of control questions, because they gather quality information so easily.

Let's start with the first two Career Fit questions:

Likes and Dislikes Questions

1. Out of all the jobs you have held, which was your most favorite? Why?
2. Out of all the jobs you have held, which was your least favorite? Why?

There's not a lot to talk about with these first two. They're fairly self-explanatory and don't need much in the way of special instructions. The only thing I want to add is that you wouldn't say, "Out of all the jobs you have held… " when a person has only held one job or has never been employed; rather, if work history is limited, you can change the question to be about their favorite and least favorite tasks. It works equally well to ask about favorite and least favorite classes or about school subjects where they earned the highest and lowest grades.

I like these questions because they work well, but unlike O-SAE questions, you have a little room to change them without incurring an ill effect. Here's another option for these questions that you might like as well: If you could change one thing about your last job, what would it be? What one thing wouldn't you change?

Strengths and Weaknesses Questions

3. On your last performance evaluation, in which three areas were you rated the strongest?
4. On your last performance evaluation, tell me the two areas that you could improve upon.

For questions three and four, the strengths and weaknesses questions, there are some very specific guidelines. First, always ask about the candidate's strengths first. Ask for three strengths, then give them time to brag. This helps make the candidate feel confident. When you are ready to follow up with the question about weaknesses, downplay it. Make it seem as if you really don't care about the information, that you already like the candidate but you have to ask these questions as a formality. Don't say that, but try to come across that way. That's why you are asking for only two weaknesses. I often joke around and sometimes say something like, "I'm not sure of the current politically correct term for 'weaknesses' because it keeps changing. I think it's called 'areas of opportunity' now." Usually the candidate chuckles.

The reason we base this question on the candidate's last performance evaluation is because that makes the information less subjective. The candidate should have a copy of that evaluation, even though you are not going to ask to see it. Also, a reference check with a prior boss could easy substantiate what the candidate says, making it more likely they will be truthful. The standard way of asking for weakness information—"Tell me about your weaknesses"—typically doesn't reap any useful information because they can say anything they want; you've asked for their *opinion*. Many savvy job seekers have learned how to flip their answers about weakness into answers reflecting a strength, or how to avoid talking about their weaknesses altogether. You'll frequently hear nonsense answers like, "I'm a workaholic," or, "I care too much about my work."

There is also another very good reason why you ask for strengths first and weaknesses second. If you did it the other way around, it would be easy for candidates to say, "I don't remember." When you start with their strengths first that won't be an issue. They'll have no problem remembering details that make them shine. In the rare case you get a candidate who remembers their highest ratings but has selective memory loss when it comes to their lowest ratings, don't let them off the hook. Here's a technique that always works: if the candidate volleys the question back to you, stating that they just can't remember, reply by saying, "That's okay, take a moment to think about it." Here's the rule—*you must not be the one to speak next*! Do you know how long fifteen seconds of silence feels in an interview when the ball has just been placed back in your court? It feels like an eternity. To break the silence, the candidate will come up with an answer. You're sending a clear message that they can't get away with not answering interview questions. Furthermore, weakness information is valuable information. It not only tells you about any possible skill deficits a candidate may have, it tells you what they are least motivated to do. Interviewers need to remain in charge of the information-gathering process.

If no performance evaluation has occurred, it works equally well to rephrase the questions and ask them either of these ways instead:

» If we were to give your supervisor a call, what would they say your three strongest areas are?

» If your supervisor were to give an evaluation today, what would they say your two weakest areas are?

Immediately after you ask question four about the candidate's weaknesses, this locus of control question follows:

» What, if anything, have you done to improve your weaknesses?

There are typically only two very clear types of responses that come from this question. You'll see what I'm talking about when you give it a try for yourself. You will either get "I can't" answers along with their rationale for why, or you'll get "Let me tell you what I've done" answers followed with specific details. Answers to this question tend to be very distinctive. Some candidates will say something like, "I haven't been given the opportunity to work on my weakness because the boss keeps piling more on me," or, "They haven't provided me with any training." Conversely, others will tell you exactly what they did. These action-oriented answers will sound something like this: "Even though my job didn't require me to do this, I took a night class to brush up on my accounting skills." How we score candidate responses will be discussed in the upcoming two chapters. For the moment, I just want you to understand the purpose of this question, and the other locus of control question we will be discussing in a moment.

Goals Question

5. Tell me about your career goals for the next two to five years.

For question five, the goals question, the focus must be restricted to career, business, or professional goals. So, insert one of these words before the word "goal"; otherwise, you might get an answer such as "starting a family" or "buying a new car." I don't recommend extending the period of time out more than five years, as the question will lose its effectiveness. Nowadays most people are focused on accomplishing whatever is immediately ahead of them. Decades ago, we would ask candidates about their twenty-year plan—no joke. For a long time, most US businesses had a job-for-life mindset, in the era before downsizing and rightsizing became commonplace. Who knows—maybe staying with one employer for a long time will become popular again. If that should happen, simply adjust the "two to five years" to whatever is appropriate.

The second locus of control question is similar to the first. Instead of being about any action taken to improve the weakness, it's about any action taken towards achieving the goal:

» What steps, if any, have you taken toward reaching them?

Once again, it's common to get one of two very distinctive types of answers here. Since everyone has dreams, most candidates will state a specific goal of some kind. It's what comes after that's important. Some candidates will explain what's preventing them from making progress and will say something like, "Well, I have so much going on right now with everyone leaning on me to handle all of these responsibilities, it's impossible to work on my goals right now." Other candidates will say something like, "Although I haven't made much progress, I have put together a plan that outlines exactly what steps I need to take, and I have attached a timeframe to each. I have called the local college and they are sending me the paperwork to enroll in classes this fall." The latter involves small steps but forward steps nonetheless.

There isn't a problem if different interviewers ask the same candidate these questions again, because you never know when you'll get a different answer.

The MBI Interview Guide

Let's put it all together by talking about the flow of your interview and your MBI interview guide. At the top of the interview guide you should have a place to write the candidate's name, the date, the job title, and the interviewer's name. Before you jump into the interview, spend some time relaxing the candidate using the techniques discussed in Chapter 6 about getting your candidates to talk.

Once you see the signs that they're settling in, it's time to move on to work history and education. I recommend reviewing the last three jobs or ten years of work history; that's what is usually going to be the most applicable, but adjust it as you see fit. When reviewing work history, I like to start with the third-most recent job and work my way up to the current or most recent job. Working my way from the past to the present helps me to understand what brought the candidate to the interview with me today. It's important that you look at not only the year employment dates but also the months. If someone left a job in 2016 and started their next job in 2017, and first glance it may appear as if there was no break in employment over that period. But what if that person left in January 2016 and didn't start their next job until December 2017? That's almost a two-year gap. You'll want to catch this and ask for an explanation for any gaps.

It's also not uncommon to find that the first reason a person gives for leaving a job is often a generic answer, something like "for more advancement opportunity" or "more money." If you look closer, and notice that the candidate has the same job title and the same or lower salary, then something doesn't add up. Don't accept their first answer. Trust me, they're hoping you'll skip over it, especially if they are trying to hide a termination due to poor performance issues. Nobody is going to hold up a sign to help you out, informing you of what you missed; it's your responsibility as the interviewer to be a sharp investigator and dig deeper when necessary.

After work history, questions about skills and locus of control (O-SAE questions) come next, followed by the five Career Fit questions.

Finally comes the time we set aside for the candidate's question-and-answer period. We've refrained from sharing more details about the job and the candidate's questions for the end of the interview to preserve our ability to gather quality information. At the very end, you should share any applicable next steps and provide a realistic timeline of when you expect to make your decision.

And, you're done!

This wraps up Chapter 7. I know it was a big chapter, but keep this information fresh in your head as we move into the next two chapters on assessing and scoring candidates.

Chapter 8
How to Assess Locus of Control

Before we get started I want double-check that you've read Part I, the chapters on understanding how high performers achieve better results. If you've skipped around and arrived here without reading those chapters first, go back and read them before proceeding. One of the many reasons MBI works better than any of its predecessors is because assessing and scoring candidates is common sense when you understand what truly sets performance levels apart.

Objective Listening

Prior to jumping in with both feet to assessing and scoring locus of control, we need to cover some essentials. First and foremost, the interviewer's ability to listen is crucial. Not just any kind of listening will do. What's required is objective listening. Don't miss the word "objective," because it's important. We tend to think our listening skills are just fine, even when they're not. I can't help but think about the communications exercise where one person quietly shares a story to another and then it's repeated by whispers down the line until the last person shares it out loud. In the end, the story always sounds very different from the original.

In the interview process, when interviewers lose objectivity it's like wearing horse blinders—we have only limited vision. Losing objectivity is where prejudices, biases, and stereotyping tend to slip in. We have a feeling that we like or don't like a candidate, but we can't exactly put our finger on why. Lack of objectivity alone can sabotage the effectiveness of any interviewer or any organization's hiring process. When it happens, it can interfere with how we listen and what we hear. We only seem to hear the information that validates our viewpoint, and the rest we ignore or miss. Often, people don't even realize they've lost their objectivity.

There's also something called the halo effect, which occurs when an interviewer uses only a small piece of candidate information, either good or bad, to overshadow the entire body of facts about the candidate. The result can be that a potentially good candidate is assumed to be a bad one based on a small piece of information and is turned away. It's even worse when the opposite happens and a bad candidate is hired based on one or two pieces of positive information that don't represent the whole.

Here are some good rules to follow:

» Allow the candidate to do the majority of the talking and focus on listening to what they are saying.
» Don't make up your mind too early in the interview process.
» Continue to listen objectively throughout the entire interview until all the information is in.
» Base your decision on solid information and not on a feeling that you can't explain.
» Remind yourself that hiring based on a feeling would never stand up in court if challenged.

Being an objective interviewer is the best way to uncover the information you need to make a sound hiring decision. If you have a bad feeling about a candidate, and if that feeling has merit, the reason why will come out when conducting an effective interview. If that feeling has no merit, however, nothing will be there to substantiate it. The good or bad feeling that you get once in a while is normal, but keep in mind that it's *not* always accurate. It can be wrong. After years of experience interviewing candidates, I've had plenty of times my own gut feeling kicked in. When a strong feeling occurs in either direction—especially early on in the interview—and you don't have enough candidate information to warrant the feeling, I caution you not to read too much into it. I recall one candidate I didn't particularly care for but who had everything else pointing to him being a good hire. After a thorough reference check was done, he was hired. He turned out to be a superstar. I don't know anyone whose gut feeling has ever been 100 percent correct. I don't think you are going to change that trend either. After all, we are talking about predicting the future performance of people we hardly know. Don't be closed off to the fact that your feeling about a candidate could be without merit. Conduct an effective interview. Don't go running off on a tangent based on a feeling and lose track of gathering quality candidate information.

A Refresher on Locus of Control

This chapter is devoted to determining whether a candidate is more internally or externally motivated. Is their attitude one that is more conducive to overcoming obstacles in order to achieve good results, or is it one that believes many obstacles are insurmountable and beyond solution? Since we covered attitude and locus of control a while ago, in Chapters 2 and 3, I want to start off with a brief refresher.

A person's locus of control, or perceived control, doesn't always coincide with reality. While one person believes something is possible, another believes that very same thing can't and won't happen. Both cannot be correct; something can't be both possible and impossible at the same time.

So, which type of thinking—positive or negative, perceiving control or not perceiving it—is more accurate or corresponds closest to reality? Let's look at some of the things that were thought to be impossible in the past that in reality were not. The building of the Golden Gate Bridge broke records thought to be architecturally impossible. Running the four-minute mile, once viewed as being physically impossible, really wasn't. How about the pyramids, man in flight, moonwalks, radio, heart transplants, microwave ovens, laptop computers, and cell phones that ring no matter where we are? You get the picture. I'm sure none of these great accomplishments are attributed to any nonbelievers.

Motivational speaker and self-development author Brian Tracy said, "The predominant quality of successful people is optimism." Optimism is a quality associated with high performers. Only those who possess a positive attitude can truly grasp what's possible. They have the most accurate perception of reality. Negative thinkers cannot conceive all that can be achieved, leaving them disconnected from the truth of what can be.

> If desired results are going to happen, they happen when people try, not when they don't.

Low performers don't actually lack control to produce desired outcomes, they just think and behave like they do. Low performers have merely relinquished their control by virtue of their own thought process and therefore don't see a payoff for expending effort. Conversely, high performers realize the control they actually have, and believe that expending the effort has a potential to pay off, so they try. If desired results are going to happen, they happen when people try, not when they don't. Perception of control is clearly powerful. Because people's thinking varies on this topic, and because this variance can be exposed during an interview, interviewers can evaluate future performance based on assessment of perceived control.

A job candidate's locus of control affects how they view and respond to obstacles. Those perceiving control think about what can be done to achieve the goal. These people can speak precisely about their decision to act, their reasoning, and everything that followed. Only when candidates have expended effort can they talk in detail about the actions they took. On the other hand, when candidates believe they lack control, they aren't contemplating what action to take because they believe taking any action won't have much of an impact. These individuals cannot speak in detail about the steps they took or the effort involved because none took place. What they can talk about with great ease, however, is their rationale for why they didn't try or why they gave up. In the face of adversity, all candidates will express their belief about the control they had or lacked. The difference between these two perspectives will be noticeable.

Words Full of Meaning, or Meaningless Words?

I once watched a television interview with the famous singer Andrea Bocelli. The conversation centered on his New York stage performance. Instead of standing in front of an audience and just singing remarkably, this time he had to act. It included walking over to a bookcase and taking a book from a shelf, moving about the stage, and kissing the leading lady, all while singing opera. It doesn't sound all that difficult until you consider the fact that he is blind and had no acting experience. His focus was not on whether this was possible or on how difficult it would be to pull off, but on how he was going to do it. Without an extensive vocabulary in English, he quoted the saying, "Where there's a will, there's a way," and because his focus was on finding a way—he did. It's not the quote that's important, but rather, the action that followed.

Reciting an inspirational quote doesn't distinguish the high performer from the rest. If that were the case, inspirational quotes would be the first thing low performers would say during a job interview. In the Information Age, guidance on how to ace an interview is available within seconds.

Technically, what candidates say during an interview comes with no guarantee. Know that anyone can say anything. The fact that words are spoken doesn't make them true and absolute. Con artists use words as tools of deception but have nothing to back them up. They make their living by convincing people of something that isn't actually so. They have mastered the art of the spoken word. Some candidates have mastered this as well. I'm not suggesting in any way that candidates are con artists, but some of them do manage to convince their interviewers that there is no one better to hire when, in fact, there is. In an interview, some words that are spoken are genuine and meaningful, others are only well intended, and some words are spoken only for the purpose of encouraging a job offer. It can be difficult to tell the difference between meaningful or meaningless words.

When words are full of meaning, they are backed with matching action. There are no contradictions between what is said and what was done. When words and actions correspond, they are congruent, meaning they are consistent and in harmony with each other. They equal each other. When a candidate expresses a desire to achieve a goal but has taken no action, or took action for a short time and gave up, or did something entirely different, there is a discrepancy between the candidate's words and their behavior; they are incongruent.

When I was a corporate recruiter, I remember interviewing this young woman who told me that she really wanted the opportunity to be promoted from an hourly employee to a manager. She said that she liked the company, wanted to stay, and was interested in moving up. It was a good conversation, and I was aware that she did a good job as an hourly paid employee. As we talked further, I found out that she did not have her high school diploma or her GED. I told her this was a requirement for management, which it was, and I said we would seriously consider her if she met this requirement. Now the ball was in her court and she needed to take action. Her words sounded gung ho, but I never heard back from her. She talked about wanting to move into management but never followed through to make it happen. Getting her GED was an obstacle that she let stand in the way of her goal. Later, I heard that she had lots of excuses for why she couldn't meet this requirement, and she said that all of them happened to be out of her control. If you noticed, her actions did not match with her eager words.

> We want employees who are self-motivated and who we can trust to take action and persist for long enough to fulfill a verbal promise.

When we are talking about overcoming obstacles and about reaching goals, for the words to be genuine, the effort that follows needs to be sustained for long enough to reach the goal. Empty words and spurts of effort just don't cut it. This reflects a lack of self-motivation. What we want instead is to hire candidates who have a pattern of follow-through integrity. We want employees who are self-motivated and whom we can trust to take action and persist for long enough to fulfill a verbal promise. This kind of integrity is made evident by having a consistent habit of keeping one's word. Integrity leads to trust. Lack of follow-through erodes trust.

Take a moment and think about how the high performer and the low performer will talk about their perceived control to overcome obstacles. Do you think they will sound exactly the same? If not, what do you think the distinctions will be? Think about your employees and how their quantity of effort and their quantity of excuses differ. It's really not hard to see when you know specifically what you're looking for. During an interview, several possible scenarios can exist regarding a candidate's words and the actions.

Scenario 1

This candidate openly expresses her perception that she lacked control. She explains why there was nothing she could do to change the outcome and says who or what was responsible. When asked to talk about her effort, she gives excuses to rationalize her lack of effort. What this candidate said and did align perfectly. Her words convey a lack of perceived control and she lacked sufficient effort.

Scenario 2

This candidate says all the right things: "Yes, yes, I have a great attitude, I am positive and upbeat!" He practically bursts out singing a few verses of Ray Stevens's "Everything Is Beautiful." Okay, maybe the last part was an exaggeration, but you get my point. His words come across like he's full of action, but the actions are absent. When asked for a specific time he dealt with an unrealistic deadline, he responds by saying that he always find a way to get his projects done and on time. When asked to share a specific time he dealt with an irate customer, again he recites doing whatever it takes to please his customers. This candidate has clearly taken an advanced course on how to become interview savvy. He has learned the art of providing good-sounding, generic answers. Sometimes these responses are long-winded replies that are full of fluff and never actually answer the question, in hope of fooling the interviewer. This candidate is attempting to come across like he's a high performer. Let's suppose this candidate is also likeable, believable, and dressed to impress. His words sound good, but the actions to back them up are nonexistent. This guy isn't as easy as you may think to spot because interviewers want to believe him, so they do.

Scenario 3

This candidate has the "yes—yes, I can do it" attitude, says all the right things and can, in fact, back up their words with a detailed account of sustained effort. Here, the words and actions are congruent in a good way. The words don't just have a positive spin, they are supported with substance: positive action. This candidate truly perceives control because their words are followed by action. Action validates and reinforces the candidate's words. Even if this candidate lacks prior experience and skills in the field and cannot offer parallel industry examples, they can still talk about other past experiences that show examples of regularly expending effort. Having a history or strong pattern of applying effort toward conquering obstacles is a crucial component for all high performers.

The first two scenarios have something in common. The words may have differed, but both lacked any detailed discussion of expended effort. It was action—or, more specifically, the lack of action—that was more revealing than the words. When faced with determining whether words or actions have more substance, choose actions, hands down. What a candidate *does* is a much better indicator than what they say.

Out of the three scenarios just discussed, the last candidate offers the greatest potential for producing the best results if hired. Your success as an interviewer comes down to accurately assessing risk and placing your bet on the candidate with the greatest probability of success.

Scoring Basics

As we know, MBI skill-assessment questions gather two pieces of information: skill and locus of control. This means we're going to do two assessments and scores *per skill question*.

The first score is for rating the candidate's skill. I recommend using a one-to-five skill-rating scale because it's simple and straightforward. It has a middle score, three, which if chosen means the candidate's level of skill is considered to be satisfactory or average. The two and four scores denote a slightly below- or above-average level of skill, and the one and five scores are unsatisfactory and excellent respectively. Directly next to the numbers are an *E* for an external locus of control rating and an *I* representing an internal locus of control rating.

When you ask a three-part O-SAE question pertaining to a specific skill, candidates will provide information about both their level of skill and their locus of control in the same answer. There is one (three-part) question and one (three-part) answer, and two assessments and scores. We don't spend any more time than this on discussing how to rate skills. Subject matter experts know what a good skill answer is and what a bad one sounds like, and should score these answers accordingly. My only word of caution is not to be too liberal handing out fives; make sure it's earned.

> I think most people realize you're supposed to stay in the game and it's not acceptable to give up, not in sports and not in the workplace.

Since assessing locus of control is new for most interviewers, that's where we're going to spend most of our time. Once we ask a candidate about a past situation involving an obstacle, the candidate will start out by sharing some of the details about their unique situation. When prompted with the A (action taken) portion of O-SAE question, they will explain what they did or did not do, and specifically how they *responded* to the obstacle. Here is where the candidate's locus of control is exposed. Things interviewers need to listen very closely for are excuses, shedding of ownership, and denial of responsibility. When control is relinquished, finger-pointing takes the place of accepting ownership: "I don't have my homework assignment to turn in and it's not my fault. The dog ate it."

Be alert for phrases such as "It will *never* change" or "It will *always* be this way" to justify inevitable doom and validate a lack of effort or quitting. In the book titled *Setback Is a Setup For a Comeback*, renowned inspirational speaker and author Willie Jolley wrote, "You may not be responsible for getting knocked down, but you're certainly responsible for getting back up." Those who don't get back up have quit trying. I think most people realize that you're supposed to stay in the game and that it's not acceptable to give up, neither in sports nor in the workplace. It especially doesn't sound good to say that you just quit trying during a job interview. For these explanations to work, they must sound legitimate and convincing— and they usually do.

Interviewers also need to watch out for the martyr or the "poor me" pitch associated with a halfhearted effort. This scenario plays out as a story of a real trooper who sadly had success snatched away by uncontrollable and unresolvable hardships. Good-sounding answers with no specific details of effort or action taken are the hallmark of external answers. Interviewers aren't judging the merits or the believability of an excuse or the size of an obstacle; instead we're judging the size of the response to the obstacles while recognizing excuses and lack of effort for what they really are: ineffective behavior.

Explanations that shift control away from oneself are the outward expression of externally perceived control. The candidate places their focus on something external that had control and prevented them from achieving their goal. You'll find that when candidates talk about being powerless and lacking control, they're *not* talking about the effort they put in or about their success. Here are some examples of expressions that show a belief in lack of control. These are usually followed by a statement of justification:

External Clues (Lacking Control)
» I couldn't. It was impossible.
» It would've never worked.
» I had no control over it.
» It failed before and will fail again.
» It wasn't meant to be.

>> It failed but that wasn't my fault.
>> It'll never change.
>> It was never going to happen. I had to give up.
>> It was doomed to fail.
>> I had no other choice.
>> There was nothing I could do about it.
>> It was just bad luck.

The locus of control assessment in MBI looks at how easily a candidate quits trying and starts making excuses when under the pressure of hardship. Excuses offer one of the biggest clues to a candidate's locus of control, and are more prevalent with those who have an external locus of control.

They're not the *only* clue however. Actions tell "the rest of the story," to use radio commentator Paul Harvey's famous phrase. Harvey would often share little-known details about highly self-motivated individuals, only to reveal their actual identity at the end. He told one story about a gentleman named James Murray Spangler, an asthmatic who was allergic to the dust generated from the carpets he swept during his nighttime job as a janitor. Spangler was so committed to making an honest living, he started tinkering on his own time with various parts including a dust pan, a broom stick, and an old pillow case. He rigged up a device that could inhale carpet dust without exhaling it. In 1907, Spangler invented the first successful portable upright electric vacuum cleaner. He later sold his patent to William Hoover, and his invention is now known to everyone as the Hoover vacuum cleaner. Spangler took action in the face of hardship and in the process he changed the world. Not bad for a janitor!

The locus of control assessment also looks for action and problem-solving efforts and the refusal to give up, all while under the pressure of hardship. These behaviors are more prevalent in those with an internal locus of control. Candidates with perceived control, or those who are internally motivated, will answer questions incorporating their optimistic "I can" attitude. When asked, they can provide a detailed description of their efforts. They have an attitude like the title character of *The Little Engine That Could*, the children's book written by Wally Piper that said, "I think I can, I think I can, I know I can, I know I can." And when the little engine made it over the mountain, it proclaimed, "I knew I could, I knew I could!"

Listen for words and phrases that are positive and that are accepting of responsibility even if success hasn't happened yet. Here are some examples of the types of phrases to listen for:

Internal Clues (Perceived Control)

» I can and I did.
» I had to find a way to do it.
» I wasn't going to give up.
» I was sure it was possible.
» I'm still working on it!
» It was difficult but I saw it through.
» We had to think of creative solutions.
» I knew I could make it work.
» I had obstacles, but I overcame them.
» I found a solution.
» Where there's a will, there's a way.
» There was an answer.

When assessing locus of control, it's important to listen to the words but judge the actions or lack thereof. Words provide the heads-up, but it's what follows that matters most because actions don't just speak louder than words, they validate the words.

Expect Both Internal and External Answers from Every Candidate

You might be thinking people either comprehend their power or they don't, and that candidates will give all internal or all external answers. If that were the case, all you would need to do as an interviewer is ask one question involving one obstacle and get one answer. That should tell you everything you need to know about the candidate's locus of control, right? Sorry. That's not the case. One locus of control answer taken on its own is only a clue, not a conclusion. It's one piece of the puzzle. We need more pieces to complete the puzzle and see the full locus of control picture.

During *every* interview I've done using MBI, I've collected both internal and external answers. This is normal. As human beings we think both ways. It's unrealistic to believe there is a person out there who *never* puts forth any effort or *never* makes an excuse. Sometimes we think "I can" thoughts and sometimes we think that we can't do it. Sometimes we see our power to invent things, to bring about change, and to achieve magnificent results, and other times we insist there's no way. An excuse by itself doesn't mean there is a rampant problem or that the candidate is externally motivated. And one specific example of taking action and expending problem-solving effort does not alone signify that a person is highly self-motivated. Assessing locus of control is not about looking for a single clue or a single way of thinking within a person but rather looking for a *pattern*. To see a pattern of behavior, interviewers must look at more than one example of behavior. By continuously asking for examples of the candidate's behavior involving an obstacle, this pattern will become visible.

Scoring

Although every candidate will give both internal and external responses, one response to an obstacle cannot be both. An answer cannot be *a little* internal and *a little* external at the same time. It's either one or the other. Here's the rule: *Only answers that provide specific problem-solving details, action, and effort taken towards overcoming the obstacle can be scored internal.* When that evidence

exists, the *I* (internal) can be circled on the interview guide next
to that answer. If matching effort and action don't accompany the
words, it cannot be scored internal. If the details aren't there, it *must*
be scored *E* (for external), regardless of the outcome. Period. End
of story.

You're going to ask candidates what the end result was, but in
the locus of control assessment you are *not* rating how it turned out.
Let me explain why. Let's say someone put forth an extreme amount
of effort. That person can talk about their problem-solving efforts
in detail, along with what they tried, what didn't work, what was
done next, who else was involved, and even the times and dates it all
happened... *even if they ultimately failed.* The locus of control score
in this example would be internal because of the detailed evidence.
Imagine interviewing Thomas Edison while he was in the process of
inventing the incandescent light bulb, which involved over 10,000
failures. Let's say the interview took place around the time he had
failed 7,500 times. He would look like a *big* failure and a low performer if we were to judge him only based on success or failure. As
interviewers, we could miss out on hiring some amazing people if
we only looked at results.

On the other hand, let's say you have a person who encountered
an obstacle and took little action, but got lucky and ended up with
a good outcome despite their lack of effort. Maybe someone did the
work for them. Regardless, the locus of control score in this case
would be external. Given the same situation, but this time with a
failed outcome, the score is the same: external. That's because we're
not scoring the outcome, but rather, the lack of specific details about
any action or problem-solving efforts.

The locus of control rating is contingent upon what happens in
between the goal being set and the outcome. It's whatever is sand-
wiched in the middle. Scoring based on results only takes the outcome into account and doesn't provide for the candidate's attitude,
actions, or thought process behind the scene. MBI requires that we
assess how the candidate arrived at the outcome. If someone puts

in a lot of effort and is worthy of an internal locus of control score, but ultimately fell short of the goal, you can lower the skill score if you feel like they did not do enough to achieve success, but not the locus of control rating.

> The locus of control rating is contingent upon what happens in between the goal being set and the outcome.

Let me give you an example of that. You are interviewing a manager who tells you about a great employee who almost single-handedly improved the store's customer satisfaction rating, but she had one big problem: showing up for work on time. The manager tells you in detail all the steps he took to get the employee to show up on time. He asked her (the employee) if she needed a schedule change or if she had a personal issue she wanted to share that was preventing her from arriving on time. He set her up with a mentor. When that didn't work, he gave her a verbal warning, followed by a formal written warning. When nothing worked, he ended up terminating the employee. With all of the specific detail regarding his efforts, an internal locus of control score is warranted. You may believe he failed because he didn't save an employee who provided some of the best customer service, however. If you happen to think he didn't do enough, then give him a lower skill score on dealing with an employee performance issue, *but keep the internal rating intact*. I happen to believe he did everything he could and even went the extra mile for her. The way I see it is that it's the employee's responsibility to get to work on time.

In an MBI workshop, we put a great deal of emphasis on teaching attitude and locus of control. In addition to a video on the power of attitude in the workplace, attendees listen to songs and assess the lyrics for locus of control, and participate in interactive and group exercises. During an interview video we present this exact scenario and occasionally someone will say, "I would have liked to see him do more to save the otherwise good employee." Whichever viewpoint is yours, I want to make certain you fully comprehend how to score locus of control correctly.

Three Reasons Why Assessing Results Is Not Recommended

Using a candidate's past track record of results to predict future performance isn't always effective and is not recommended. Using results exclusively to evaluate a candidate is flawed on a number of levels. First, as we just pointed out, if a person hasn't succeeded yet but they are still pursuing the goal, we would shortchange this candidate because their record lacks sufficient results. Second, if a person hasn't been given an opportunity to showcase their abilities but would relentlessly pursue great results once given the chance, there will also be no results to measure. This candidate may well be a high performer, but if judged on results alone, they would also be excluded from consideration. Third, if the goal was easily attainable, you won't know whether you have a high performer or not. You won't know if this candidate will give up when the going gets tough.

Failure from Another Perspective

Why don't we judge failures? Don't we want to hire people who succeed more and fail less? Aren't low performers associated with failure? It's time to change how we think about failure. Let's look at failure from another perspective. Failure technically hasn't happened until a person throws in the towel. Defeat cannot be acknowledged while a person is still trying. For a high performer, failure is more like a "success in progress." For low performers, it's very different.

Failures, for them, are the uncontrollable and insurmountable final outcome. They are the reason effort is aborted. *It's not really failure that's the big issue, it's more about how much effort was put in and about abandoning effort.* Knowing the difference between a failure that is a normal part of the process of achievement versus a failure that stems from a breakdown in the process—quitting—is a critical distinction that's necessary for identifying performers.

Determining Predominant Locus of Control

Now we are getting down to the nitty-gritty. A candidate's locus of control responses are amassed over the entire interview. An appreciable amount of behavior is examined and then linked together to create a pattern of behavior and a bigger picture. If any answer doesn't seem clear-cut to you as one way or the other and you are unsure how to score it, then don't score it. For those that are apparent, *every* one of them must be counted, whether it's what you wanted to hear or not. Assessing locus of control entails tallying of all the candidate's locus of control responses to adversity, and determining which type of perceived control occurred more often, internal or external. In MBI, this is called the candidate's predominant locus of control.

A behavior pattern that more often shows a candidate as perceiving control and focused on possibility points to a person who is predominantly internally motivated. A pattern of behavior that more often reflects the abandonment of control and is focused on impossibility, limitations, and excuses shows that the person is predominantly externally motivated. The less varied a candidate's responses are between internal and external—or rather, the greater the occurrence of one type of response—the stronger that person adheres to whatever perspective they believe.

High performers are those people who most often embrace the power of positive thinking and then expend the effort to prove that their optimistic way of thinking is correct. It really is the same process with the low performer as it is with the high performer—the process of proving one's perception of control to be right. The high performer proves that they are right by expending the effort and not quitting until they achieve the desired outcome, proving that their perception of control is correct. The low performer withholds action and limits the supply of self-motivation to prove their perception of control correct. Henry Ford, the American automobile manufacturer, created the Ford Model T in 1908 and improved on the assembly line mode of production, which revolutionized the automotive industry. As a result, Ford sold millions of cars and became a world-famous company head. Clearly, he knew what he was talking about when he said, "Whether you think you can, or you think you can't—you're right." High performers and low performers have differences and similarities. The main difference is that high performers think they can and low performers think they can't. They are similar in the aspect that they both believe they are right and they both work to prove their thinking right.

There Is No Tie

When it comes to determining predominant behavior, I want you to realize something that you cannot do. Let's say for the moment that you are assessing a candidate's skill level on a scale of one to five, with five being the highest or best rating. What would a three rating for a skill mean? It would denote average skill level, right? And it's correct to say that average would be an admissible rating. Now, if the candidate provided an equal amount of internal and external responses, what would their predominant response be? Would it be average? Half and half denotes neither one as being predominant. It offers us no relevant information and therefore cannot be used. *When determining a candidate's predominant locus of control there is no such thing as a tie.* To prevent the possibility of a tie, I recommend that you always ask an odd number of O-SAE questions. Whatever the case, should you happen to get stuck with an equal amount of each type of response, go into overtime until you break the tie. Ask for a few more past behavior examples involving more obstacles. At some point you will have amassed enough information to establish a predominant locus of control.

The other thing you can't do is make up your mind too soon. Throughout the entire interview process, the candidate will verbalize his or her perception of control. So, let's say you've asked four interview questions so far and all of the candidate's responses are external. That can't make you feel very confident about the viability of the candidate, much less that they are a high performer. Maybe you're even considering ruling this candidate out and ending the interview early. *Don't.* Let's say you have seven remaining questions. The candidate could provide internal answers to every one of them. You can't know until you ask. Even though both internal and external responses are common to all candidates, there's no formula to the order they come out. If you make up your mind before all the evidence is in, you'll lose objectivity.

OK... It's Time to Practice!

I'm going to give you some candidate answers to an O-SAE question (just the O-S part) for customer service, and I want you to assess each answer's locus of control. I'm telling you in advance that I'm going to provide an answer that has an excuse or blaming, one that's a good-sounding generic answer, and one with specific details—but not necessarily in that order. I want you to assess the locus of control only and not the skill. I also want to make sure you can clearly distinguish between these three different types of answers.

Question 1
Tell me about a specific time when you dealt with an irate customer.

Candidate Answer 1

Working in retail, I get a lot of rude customers. They're often very demanding and have unrealistic expectations. Some want refunds without having a receipt. They can get pretty angry when they don't get their way. But I tell them my hands are tied and there's nothing I can do about it. It's the company policy.

I or E? Why? _____

Candidate Answer 2

Whenever I have irate customers, I try to pull them aside so other customers don't hear them in case they raise their voice. I listen and find out what the problem is. Then I usually apologize, ask them what I can do to make them happy, and do it.

I or E? Why? _____

Candidate Answer 3

A customer came in with a pressure washer he had purchased from us about six months ago. It had stopped working. He wanted a refund, but I wasn't able to do that. I explained that after ninety days it becomes a warranty issue. I offered him a 20 percent discount but that didn't make him happy. I called my district manager to find out if there was anything I could do, but I was told the discount was it. I ended up looking up the direct phone number to the manufacturer's warranty department and printed him a copy of his receipt. I thought that might help him a little. I also suggested that he consider buying a new unit, one that was more heavy-duty since he used this equipment almost daily for work. He seemed to understand and be okay.

I or E? Why? _____

Let's see how you did. The first two answers are external, and the third one is internal. Did you get them all right? Did you catch the powerless "it's not my fault and there's nothing I can do about it" attitude in the first answer? Did you notice the no-try aspect as well? There are often solutions, or at least other options to explore, but this candidate seemed unwilling to go there. How about the second candidate's answer? Did you pick up on the fact it was a good-sounding generic answer that had no actual details or specifics? These types of answers always try to make the candidate sound great. Properly trained MBI interviewers don't fall for them! On answer three, did you consider the outcome a failure because the customer wanted a refund and didn't get it? If yes, did you let it sway your locus of control rating? I hope not. Most importantly, did you notice the problem-solving effort and action the candidate took, and how he was able to talk about it in specific detail? He had a real-life example: a specific customer with a specific issue. He shared what the product was and provided additional specifics regarding the actions he took. What we had was the same question answered three different ways. Don't think that any of these answers are unrealistic or that candidates won't actually provide them, because they are all inspired by actual interviews.

Let's try a few more.

Question 2
Tell me about a specific time when you felt overwhelmed with your workload or job demands.

Candidate Answer
I can handle a lot at one time. I always try to do things one at a time to produce the best results. (I or E?)

Question 3
Tell me about a specific time when you were treated unfairly by a coworker or boss.

Candidate Answer

I applied for a shift leader position several times. I never got it because of office politics and favoritism that benefited other people but never me. (I or E?)

Question 4

Tell me about a time when you felt it was okay to go outside company policy to satisfy a customer.

Candidate Answer

A lady had a flat tire and wanted it patched rather than replacing the tire. I wasn't allowed to do that but what I did instead was put the spare tire on the car for her. (I or E?)

The locus of control on questions two and three is external. How about for question four? Did you score the locus of control? When interviewers get the locus of control assessment wrong, it's typically due to one the following three reasons: The first one happens when interviewers get fooled by good-sounding generic answers with no specific details of action taken, and score them internal because they sound so good. The second one happens when interviewers rate an outcome instead of the effort that was put forth. Said another way, it happens when only successes are scored internal and only failures are given an external locus of control score. That's not how it works.

The third reason applies to question four above. Some interviewers ask ineffective interview questions (i.e., no obstacle, no "specific," etc.) that cannot elicit locus of control information, but they score locus of control anyway. Go back and read the fourth question. Where's the obstacle? Where's the word "specific"? Why is there the leading, happily ending outcome, "to satisfy a customer"? That question is a mess. It fails to meet the criteria and therefore doesn't even qualify as being an MBI question. That's means you can't even assess locus of control using question four. When we don't ask for the specifics, we cannot distinguish between who has the details and who doesn't. The obstacle is the fork in the road in the process of achievement that exposes a person's real attitude. *Without the obstacle we cannot assess locus of control.* It's crucial to use properly constructed O-SAE questions if we expect to get the assessment right. Remember, we're not in the Wild West anymore. MBI has rules, and if you don't follow them, it won't work!

> **Without the obstacle we cannot assess locus of control.**

Do you remember those two lone locus of control questions woven into the Career Fit questions in the Chapter 7? The first question follows the weakness question and asks what, if anything, the candidate has done to improve upon their weaknesses. The second one follows the goal questions and asks what steps, if any, the candidate has taken towards reaching the goal. I mentioned that the answers to these locus of control questions tend to be very distinctive. How would you score the answers to the weakness and goal locus of control questions below?

Question 5
What have you done, if anything, to improve your weaknesses?

Candidate Answer 1
Even though my job didn't require me to do this, I took a night class to brush up on my accounting skills. (I or E?)

Candidate Answer 2
They haven't provided me with any training. (I or E?)

Candidate Answer 3

I haven't been given the opportunity to work on my weakness because the boss keeps piling more on me. (I or E?)

Question 6

What steps, if any, have you taken toward reaching your career goals?

Candidate Answer 1

Well, I have so much going on right now with everyone leaning on me to handle all of these responsibilities, it's impossible to work on my goals right now. (I or E?)

Candidate Answer 2

Although I haven't made much progress, I have put together a plan that outlines exactly what steps I need to take, and I have attached a timeframe to each. I have called the local college and they are sending me the paperwork to enroll in classes this fall. (I or E?)

Answer one for the question five and two for the question six are internal responses, and the rest are external responses. We're about at the end of this chapter and ready to move on to assessing and scoring Career Fit, but before we do there is one more important topic we need to address—the effect of the interviewer's locus of control on the interview process.

The Interviewer's Locus of Control

The more someone is externally motivated, the more they will use excuses and rationalize their inability to move forward rather than figure out how to achieve a goal. But you already know this. What you may not have realized is sometimes these people become interviewers and make hiring decisions for their organization.

The more we use excuses, and the more we believe in their legitimacy, the more we accept them from others and buy into them as being valid reasons for inaction and failure. *Interviewers with an external locus of control can more easily become sympathetic and understanding toward responses they can personally relate to.* This can cause interviewers to score answers incorrectly—more specifically, to mark external responses as internal.

It is unrealistic to think that every interviewer possesses a high degree of internal locus of control. Organizations with interviewers who struggle to achieve good hiring results, even after MBI training, often have to face the reality that some of their interviewers are not high performers. This adds an extra dimension to the hiring process. We not only need to consider the locus of control of the candidates we are interviewing and contemplating hiring, we also need to consider the locus of control of those we allow to conduct interviews. *Organizations need to make sure they have the right people making their hiring decisions.*

On to Chapter 9.

Chapter 9
How to Assess Career Fit

Many candidates who lack a high level of interest in a job are hired and then coerced into shifting their passion to fit the job. Let's face it, there's an expectation that all new hires are, or at least should be, highly motivated. Managers are often surprised when they discover that a share of their employees aren't motivated, and they don't understand why so many appear to be indifferent about the very job they seemed so eager to get. So, now what? We may not be able to fix the employees whom we've already hired, but we can certainly address the role we played in hiring employees who aren't high performers.

Bad Person or Wrong Occupation?

What is a *bad hire*, anyway? Is it a bad person? Are we talking about the employee's quality of character? Do we mean that the person is either good or bad? Could it be that a bad hire is really a good person but is someone who has made a not-so-good career choice, and that in the right job this employee would have been a good hire? Absolutely. When we're talking about a good or a bad hire, we are talking about the degree to which an employee performs their job. It's their *performance* that we are classifying as being either good or bad, not the person.

Every human being, without exception, has the potential to reach great personal heights. The most crucial part of personal achievement, and for some people the most difficult part, is figuring out what it is they really want to be doing. Just because candidates haven't figured it out yet doesn't mean the interviewer can't assess passion or identify high performers.

Many years ago, I conducted an exit interview on a retail manager. The company decided to demote a struggling manager back to an hourly employee just a little more than a year after promoting him. The company spent the prior six months working with him in an attempt to improve his job performance, but their efforts were unsuccessful. Instead of being demoted, however, this manager (I'll call him Mike) chose to leave the company and accept another career opportunity elsewhere. Mike accepted a new job as a manager at a video store just down the road.

During the exit interview, Mike confessed that what he really wanted to do was pursue a career in computers. According to his supervisor, Mike's performance suffered in the areas of employee and customer relations. Mike also expressed personal frustration with both of those areas. He really disliked the constant requests for special days off from employees and he especially disliked dealing with any customer who had a complaint. His job required that he spend most of his time on the front line. Not surprisingly, Mike instead drifted to the back of the store and spent most of his time there, behind the scenes, away from people, doing inventory and working on developing a custom computer program that would augment a corporate marketing campaign—a task he took the initiative to do even though it wasn't part of his job. Naturally, he gravitated toward what he enjoyed doing while avoiding those areas he disliked. It's human nature.

Mike wasn't a bad person or a lazy person. On the contrary, there was a reason he was promoted into management in the first place. He was a conscientious employee. For the most part, however, this job required that Mike do mostly tasks that he disliked and only a few he enjoyed. Just like anyone else, he took the most initiative in areas that interested *him* the most. Unfortunately, Mike's area of interest was different from what the company was most interested in having him do. The problem was that Mike wasn't right for the job, or the job wasn't right for Mike, depending how you look at it. The job as a retail manager wasn't a good match with Mike's likes, strengths, or goals.

Mike chose to continue his career in retail management at the video store because he lacked the education or experience needed to get hired right away as a computer programmer. And I am sure the person who interviewed and hired him at this video store did so because of his past retail management experience. This interviewer was correct in thinking that Mike could do the job. But a job change to another company where he would do similar work would not fix the problem Mike was having with his job performance. The majority of the responsibilities that his new job required were the same things he disliked in his previous job: dealing with employee and customer issues.

Mike first got his start in retail when a friend of his told him about a job opening where the friend was employed. His friend highly recommended both the job and the company to Mike, and recommended Mike to his manager who was hiring at the time. Mike was interviewed and extended a job offer on the spot. Now Mike has work experience in this industry to put on his résumé, making it easier for him to move to other retail jobs.

That's not where the story ends. Mike kept in touch with me for a while. After working at the video store for a few months, he figured out for himself that he was in the wrong type of work. He also managed to find a way to go back to school and get a degree in computer science—which was what he really wanted to be doing the most! The last time we spoke, he was doing great. He said he was no longer working in retail and had landed a job as a programmer. Mike's prior issue with poor performance had evaporated, and he was now excelling in his new career. Best of all, he loved the work he was doing. Hiring people to do jobs that aren't right for them is not a good practice for any organization, but it's also no picnic for their employees.

It's not a coincidence that Mike's job performance issues paralleled exactly with his likes and dislikes. He acquired the necessary skills to do his job, but his retail jobs consisted mainly of tasks that were contrary to what motivated him the most. Nobody's motivation level is intensified by performing tasks they don't like to do.

Yes, high performers love their work! They are personally interested in it and want to be doing it. It motivates them and they bond with it. Loving one's chosen career is the reason high performers pour so much of themselves into doing their jobs. Candidates may have the right attitude to achieve and even the right skill set to do the job, but if they are lacking a bona fide interest in it, their performance won't be on par with that of high performers. A high level of interest is required to amplify self-motivation to the level of a high performer. What a candidate loves to do must be a match with the duties and responsibilities of the job. As you will remember (from Chapter 4), when this match occurs it's called Career Fit.

> Nobody's motivation level is intensified by performing tasks they don't like to do.

Think of a person laden with passion who wants to be a computer programmer, like Mike. Think of this person as being akin to an electrical outlet on a wall. He is ready and able to transfer energy, but in order for this energy or self-motivation to flow, he needs someplace to dispense it. He needs an electrical cord to plug in and tap into his energy. The candidate is the wall outlet and the right job plugs into the socket and the energy is unleashed into the organization. Realize, not every plug will fit every socket. There is more than one type of each. Receptacles can be 110 or 220 volts, they can be grounded or not, and polarized or not. They can be a three-phase outlet, 12-volt DC, 50 or 60 Hz—get the point? For the maximum energy to flow, there must be a good electrical connection.

Figure 9.1. Plugging in

This means the plug and the outlet must be the same type. High performers have simply found the right match for them, in the form of a job.

Let me share a real story that bolsters this analogy. I remember having to replace a clothes dryer that quit working. When the new dryer arrived I discovered, to my dismay, that I had one type of 220-volt electrical outlet and a differently shaped 220-volt plug. In my case, the problem was easily resolved by an electrician who changed the wall socket to match the plug. Unfortunately, we don't have electricians who can swap out an employee's likes and dislikes to get the energy of self-motivation to flow. I cannot overstress the importance of Career Fit assessment and incorporating it into your interviewing and hiring decision process.

Here's one more point to consider. For the person whose greatest interest is programming computers, the best outlet would be a job where they could do computer programming. This means the similarities between the candidate's interests and the job are identical, thus allowing the greatest motivation or current to flow. That part is clear. But did you know this current doesn't flow in just one direction? It flows back to the employee in the form of personal satisfaction and fulfillment that comes from doing what they love. When organizations get this piece of hiring right, this reciprocating flow manifests itself through a natural reduction in turnover and an improvement in productivity. It's a win-win all the way around.

We know it's unrealistic to expect employees to change who they are to fit the job. The better strategy is to hire someone who has a genuine interest in doing the type of work involved. I want to make sure this sinks in, because usually we have no trouble associating the lack of skills with lack of performance, but many struggle to comprehend the fact that the lack of interest is also connected to poor performance. Unlike skill, low interest does not *necessarily* mean that candidates will be unable to perform the job. Because of this difference, skills are often given higher precedence in candidate selection. This is a mistake. Here's why: you can forego some or all of the required job skills if you have the ability to train, but *you cannot forego Career Fit if you want to hire high performers*. Skills can be taught, improved upon, and even forgotten. We know that skill development is ongoing. Interests are not so amenable. It's interest that feeds motivation, whereas skill lacks any authority to influence motivation. Since our focus is on how to hire high performers, a candidate's interests cannot be ignored.

The Comparison

Evaluating a match between a candidate and the job is not new. In reality, that's what hiring is all about. Interviewers gather information about the candidate's skills by asking some questions to determine level of skill. Then this skill information is compared with the duties and responsibilities of the job. The person with the best skills for the job is usually the one who is hired, right? Assessing interests is done exactly the same way. The *only* variation is that you are comparing the candidate's interests with the job instead of comparing the candidate's skills with the job. It's the same comparison but using different candidate information. You will be using the five specific Career Fit questions we presented earlier to gather this information. And because you already know enough about the job to be able to compare the candidate's skills with it, you'll have no problem also comparing the candidate's interests to the job. With skills, you are assessing whether the candidate *is able* to do the job. With interests, you are assessing whether they really *want* to do it. That's the difference.

The Career Fit assessment allows us not only to assess seemingly qualified candidates but also to include candidates we otherwise would not include, and that's particularly great in an industry which is starving for quality candidates. If candidates are underqualified at the time of your job opening, they could still be potentially great hires and future high performers, given the appropriate training. Rather than instantly ruling out these candidates, you can switch your focus from skill assessment to Career Fit assessment. We must determine if the job you are willing to train someone to do is the type of job the candidate would be self-motivated to do. Who knows, you may discover people who are highly motivated and are seeking an organization who will invest in them. This scenario can have better results than if you hired someone who is skilled but lacks the interest and motivation to do the job.

The Five Questions Refresher

Now, do you remember those five questions we use to assess interest level? Well, it's okay if you don't yet. Before you know it, you'll be asking them to every candidate out of habit. Let's bring them back now.

Likes and Dislikes:
1. Out of all the jobs you have held, which was your most favorite? Why?
2. Out of all the jobs you have held, which was your least favorite? Why?

Strengths and Weaknesses:

3. On your last performance evaluation, in which three areas were you rated the strongest?

4. On your last performance evaluation, tell me the two areas that you could improve upon.

Goals:

5. Tell me about your career goals for the next two to five years.

Obtaining information about interests involves asking each candidate these five questions, pertaining to *likes, dislikes, strengths, weaknesses,* and *goals.* Answers will fall into one of two groups. The first group will consist of candidate answers that reference their likes, strengths, and goals. They represent what motivates a candidate or what they will be most self-motivated to do. These are questions one, three, and five. The second group will consist of the candidate's dislikes and weaknesses. Conversely, these represent what a person is least motivated to do; they are demotivators. This information will be based on the answers to questions two and four. Both groups of questions are required to build a sufficiently complete picture of what does and does not motivate a candidate.

Likes and goals are the strongest of the indicators of what interests a candidate the most. Strengths are important indicators as well, and should align with likes and dislikes. Most people are better at doing the things they like than they are at doing the things they dislike. It's easy to obtain this information because most people enjoy talking about their special aptitude—it's a topic they know well! You can even ask children and watch them light up when they talk about what they can do well. People never lose this enthusiasm. Ideally, we want a candidate's likes, strengths, and goals to align with the duties and responsibilities of the job.

Asking candidates about their least favorite job, and why it was their least favorite, can help uncover the type of work they dislike. Weaknesses also tend to reflect dislikes. The exception is when someone states that they have great interest in pursuing and developing a particular area in which there has been no opportunity to do so as of yet. For those who have had plenty of opportunity and haven't developed the skill into a strength, it's likely that particular area doesn't hold a high-level interest to them. For example, you won't see me chasing any opportunity to learn more about accounting. It's not my strength or my interest. I know enough to get by and that's it.

Now that you have those five questions back in your head, let's talk scoring.

Scoring: Match or Mismatch

The Career Fit scoring involves a brand-new rating system. It is scored *match* and *mismatch*. They aren't abbreviated like the *I* and *E* in the locus of control scoring; they are spelled out. When a candidate's answer to the likes, strengths, and goals questions align with a part of doing the job, score that answer "match." When the answer has nothing to do with the job, the score is "mismatch." That means the candidate won't get to do what they love on this job. Next, if the dislike and weakness answers are *not* job duties, score those as a "match." Do you understand why? It's because *the job doesn't involve doing what the candidate doesn't like to do,* and that's a good thing. It's a match. Conversely, if the job entails work that the candidate strongly dislikes, or is least motivated to do, then it's scored "mismatch." When you finish scoring all five Career Fit questions, you should have a combination of five match or mismatch scores.

Technically there are no good or bad, or right or wrong, answers to the Career Fit questions. After all, how can someone's favorite job be *wrong*? We're just talking about comparing one candidate's answers to one job. The tasks, duties, and responsibilities in and of themselves are neither enjoyable nor distasteful. What makes them one way or the other is how the candidate feels about doing them.

I caution you not to put a label on a task (or job) as being good or bad, likeable or not. Your opinion isn't relevant and will only cloud matters. What one person finds enjoyable is not necessarily something everyone will. Because it is an individual preference, all candidates must be fully evaluated for their own interests.

Predominant: Liked More or Disliked More?

When we assess locus of control, we are looking for one of two outcomes: predominantly internal or predominantly external motivation. Similarly, when you assess Career Fit, you are looking for one of two outcomes. All you really need to know is whether there is a predominant match between the candidate's interests and the job or not. Just as when assessing locus of control, no single answer will provide a definitive conclusion. When determining predominant response, we must ask all of the Career Fit questions first and then step back and look at all of the information. To determine predominance, one must look at the entire body of evidence.

When a job consists mostly of tasks that the candidate views as tedious, disliked, or not enjoyable, we refer to this as a predominant mismatch. Conversely, when the job consists of tasks that align more closely with a candidate's likes, strengths, and goals, we refer to this as a predominant match. In order to tap into and use this power, there must be an absolute minimum of 51 percent match between the candidate's interests and the job. The candidate who has many of their interests correspond to the day-to-day job duties has the added benefit of the all-powerful motivating influence of interest. Since there's an odd number of Career Fit questions, there is no risk of a tie. Ultimately what we want is a person who likes doing the job more than they dislike doing it—the more, the better.

One time I came very close to having that perfect job match—that is, for *me*. I was responsible for overhauling a company's hiring process. I even had a great assistant, Connie, who would do my expense reports. For me, this job consisted of doing 99.9 percent of the things I personally loved to do. I could eat, drink, and sleep this job and work at it almost around the clock. I was so motivated! Normally, however, most jobs include a more diverse combination of a person's likes and interests, along with their least favorite and not-so-good-at tasks—a combination of matches and mismatches. This particular job was a predominant match for me. It perfectly complemented my strengths, my highest interests, and my professional goals at the time. It also did not require me to achieve in areas of weakness or lack of interest. My job and my passion were truly one and the same. I was so gung ho to do that job that I was willing to do whatever it took to do great work. I even chose to sacrifice some of my personal life to spend more time working, because I was doing exactly what I loved to do. On out-of-state recruiting trips, sometimes I wouldn't arrive home until midnight, but I'd be back at work at 9 a.m. This was my all-time favorite job, before I started what I'm doing now.

> When I look back at each job I've had, I can see a direct parallel between my interest level in that job and my motivation level to do it.

When I look back at each job I've had, I can see a direct parallel between my interest level in that job and my motivation level to do it. I remember one particular job that I stayed in for only a very short time. It was a terrible match for me because it was composed mostly of tasks I hated doing. It probably consisted of 20 percent or less of things I liked to do. I didn't enjoy the work, none of my goals were being met, and I wasn't very motivated. I couldn't wait for the end of each day to arrive, and I couldn't wait until I got another job so I could quit. I wish I had known then what I know now. I would have known better than to accept that job.

One time while I was sitting in on an interview, a candidate expressed that his least favorite part of his current job was working on designing web pages. He didn't like doing that part of his job very much. Is this a good or a bad answer? As previously mentioned, in and of itself it is neither right nor wrong. For this information to be of use, it needs to be applied to a specific scenario. Once it is, then it takes on meaning. It just so happened that this candidate was interviewing for a job that was about 95 percent website design. So how much of a match is there between this candidate and this job? Now that you know what the job is and have a basis for comparison, the information takes on meaning.

I know right about now you're asking, "What candidate would shoot himself in the foot by saying that?" It's a great question. This demonstrates the power of using the effective information gathering techniques taught in Chapter 6 to collect authentic candidate information. This candidate was screened prior to the interview and was found to have the necessary qualifications to do this job. He had prior experience with information systems, along with the skills to write applications and design websites. His résumé looked satisfactory for the job and he had enough experience and technical skill to talk about what he had done and was able to do. The candidate had good communication skills and interviewed well up to this point.

For this particular job, designing web pages was only a temporary project, but it was going to be a big portion of the job for the next year or so. When the project was finished, the job would include many other responsibilities, ones this candidate actually would like doing. This one-year project, however, was very important. It would have tight deadlines and there was a lot of work to be done. The candidate selected would need to be highly self-motivated and would have to hit the ground running—no excuses.

Since web page design was so important and also 95 percent of this job for the next year or more, it was fairly easy to conclude that a match did not exist between this candidate and this job. However, some of you might be stuck in your old hiring mindset and thinking, "Well, as long as he could do the job, who cares about the other stuff?" If you are, I would encourage you to reconsider your position, because you are ignoring the profound impact that interest level has on job performance.

Where This Assessment Can Go Wrong

Do you remember those two locus of control questions included in the Career Fit questions? The first one, the one that follows the weakness question, tends to confuse some interviewers. Let's say a candidate shares two weaknesses (from her last performance evaluation) and they are "budget preparation" and "report writing." Then you ask, "What, if anything, have you done to improve your weaknesses?" She goes on to share the specific details of the steps she took to improve both weaknesses to the point that they are now skills. The response she gave about the steps she took is a locus of control answer. I want to emphasize that. Some interviewers intertwine the two responses. If budget preparation or report writing are indeed job requirements, the Career Fit score should be *mismatch*. If you misinterpret the action taken in the locus of control answer as being a Career Fit answer, the weakness now looks like a skill, and some interviewers incorrectly score the Career Fit portion *match* instead.

Let me scream this from a rooftop! *A weakness converted into a skill is still not a passion!* Weaknesses, with or without skills, are indicators of what does *not* motivate someone. For example, I can do expenses reports. The know-how is not the problem—my lack of love for doing them is. I am notorious for procrastinating when it comes to getting my expenses reimbursed, and that hasn't changed in three decades despite my having sufficient skill to do them.

When the Stars Align

Barbara Corcoran, Shark Tank investor, summed it up in four simple words with this tweet: "You can't fake passion!"[1] When you take a closer look, you're actually getting more information about what does and does not motivate a candidate than you may realize. You may only be asking three questions related to interests and two questions related to dislikes, but you are also gathering related information from other questions throughout the interview. For example, the reason a candidate left a job can tell you about what they don't like. And the reason that person accepted a new job can provide information about what they like and what's important to them. The questions about past performance evaluation are not the only places that provide insight into strengths and weaknesses during the interview. You'll find out more when you assess the candidate's skills. The skills we rate the highest are the candidate's strengths, and the ones we rate the lowest are their weakest skills. Some candidates are quite candid about the parts of the job they loved as well as the parts they didn't. All of this information will help you build a picture of what motivates a person and can be used to compare and determine whether the candidate will be a good fit for the job you're trying to fill.

Often, we see this information aligning with and reinforcing the Career Fit answers. For example, you may find that the skills you rated the highest using O-SAE questions and the skills their last supervisor rated them the highest on their last performance evaluation are frequently similar or even identical. On the same note, the skills you rate the lowest often parallel the areas for improvement from their most recent performance evaluation. Add in their favorite job, matching their skill strengths, and their least favorite job, corresponding to their least developed skills. As you do this, all the stars start to align. What motivates a candidate and what doesn't become clear. All of the data is congruent. When that happens, it's a strong indicator that you've collected quality candidate information.

Let's also take a moment and talk about extroverts and introverts—outgoing people and task-project-process personality types. Don't confuse these personality types with internals and externals, because they have nothing to do with each other. If you pay close attention, you will notice that likes and dislikes are often indicative of a person's natural personality type. For example, people who are extroverted favor jobs that give them a chance to interact with people. In fact, you'll often find that their best skills or strengths involve interacting with people, such as providing top-notch customer service, being a good communicator, and working well with others. Their weaknesses are often in areas involving noninteractive tasks such as number crunching, data entry, or expense reports.

Introverts are just the opposite. They are most comfortable working with things, not people, such as working on a project or crunching numbers. Don't get me wrong. It's not that introverts can't work with people or that extroverts can't work on projects. Rather, introverts usually *prefer* jobs that allow them to focus more on objects or tasks. The story about Mike, the retail manager turned programmer, is a good example of an introverted high-performer.

Without knowing me personally, can you figure out which personality type I am? The clues you have so far are that I am a public speaker and trainer and my passion is interviewing and hiring. You also know that I hate doing expense reports. Yes, I am an extrovert, very much so. I never get tired of being around positive people. Because I'm on the go a lot, sometimes I feel tired when I get on stage and start speaking at a conference, but it doesn't take more than a few minutes before I feel super energized.

Personality types are not better or worse, good or bad. It's just a matter of personal preference. Everyone has their own attributes and their own contributions to make in an individual way. When we label a personality type as either good or bad, it's because we are comparing it to job requirements. If the personality type accentuates job performance, then it is good. But if it hinders job performance, it is, of course, considered bad.

Customer Service

Here's some insight I can offer, specifically in regard to customer service and hiring. I believe the biggest problem plaguing the customer service industry—and it has a big problem—is that the wrong people are being hired to do these jobs. When we talk about a compatible match between the person and the job, someone who shies away from interaction is not an ideal candidate for a job requiring a lot of interaction with customers.

I was in a grocery store one day, standing at the bakery department counter waiting for assistance. Directly behind the counter, about ten feet away, was the employee working in that department. I was the only customer there but had to wait almost five minutes before she even acknowledged me. I tried to get her attention, but she was focused on packaging muffins and never looked up. Instead of being customer focused, a necessity in this type of business, she gravitated to what she enjoyed more: a task not involving people. Sadly, it took a manager walking by to finally get her to wait on me. Whenever I feel ignored as a customer, the first thing I think is, "Who hired this person to do *this* job?"

> It's in the middle of a challenge the greatest opportunities exist—but only if you have employees who care enough to go the extra mile.

What a difference it makes having the right person in the right job. Customer service also offers many great examples of hiring done right. Some of the greatest customer service experiences I've personally had, and some I've heard others share, involved something that went wrong. But more importantly, they also included an employee who cared enough to resolve the problem in a way that created a loyal customer. It's in the middle of a challenge where the greatest opportunities exist—but only if you have employees who care enough to go the extra mile. The employees who provide that great service are merely doing what they love to do and getting paid for it. They are working in a job that is compatible with their passion. Customer service is not just about having a great policy, a great training program, or both. It is a package deal that starts with selecting the right employees. Lee Cockerell, retired Disney executive vice president who oversaw forty thousand employees, always says, "You have to hire them right, train them right, and treat them right." Amen.

By the way, if you are not familiar with Lee Cockerell, I highly recommend that you learn more about him. He's easy to find. Just Google his name or go to www.LeeCockerell.com. He shares his wisdom for free through an awesome weekly podcast on every imaginable management topic, and they are always fifteen minutes or less. I learn so much every time I listen to one; I highly recommend that you subscribe. His books are worth reading too. In *The Customer Rules*, he dedicated an entire chapter to MBI and the importance of hiring well.

It's Practice Time

Below are the five Career Fit questions along with candidate responses. This candidate is interviewing for a customer service manager position. Some of the duties and responsibilities are providing exceptional customer service, resolving customer problems and complaints, training and developing employees, supervising employees, addressing employee performance issues, scheduling employees, and demonstrating excellent listening and communication skills.

1. Out of all the jobs you have held, which was your most favorite and why?

Candidate Answer: My current job. Even though it's with a small company, I have to do a lot of different things. I love the time I get to interact with customers. I wish I could do it more.

(Match or Mismatch?)

2. Out of all the jobs you have held, which was your least favorite and why?

    Candidate Answer: Data entry clerk. Sometimes the data was unclear and there was no way I could talk to the person who owned the data to clarify it.

    (Match or Mismatch?)

3. On your last performance evaluation, in which three areas were you rated the strongest?

    Candidate Answer: Dealing with customers, employee relations, and my communication skills.

    (Match or Mismatch?)

4. On your last evaluation, tell me two areas you could improve upon.

    Candidate Answer: Budget preparation and scheduling employees.

    (Match or Mismatch?)

5. Tell me about your career goals for the next two to five years.

    Candidate Answer: To become a customer service manager with a larger organization and eventually move up. My ultimate goal, down the road, is to become a regional customer service manager.

    (Match or Mismatch?)

Let's see how you did. The candidate's first answer is a match. So is his second answer. Did you get that one right? Data entry is *not* a part of the job he is applying for, so he won't be required to do a task he dislikes, making the score a match. His strengths on his last performance evaluation match nicely with the job he is interviewing for and that makes answer three another match. How about question four? Match or mismatch? The job does require scheduling, and that's not a strength of his. Even though he may have the skill or ability to do it, it's not something he loves doing. That makes this the first mismatch score. If scheduling is only a small part of doing the job then it may not be a big deal, but the score still remains a mismatch. However, in this job, if 95 percent of the time is spent working on and scheduling employees then it is a big deal. Question five is also clearly a match.

Now let's stand back and look at the whole picture. What is this candidate's predominant Career Fit, a match or mismatch? When you tally up the five answers, four are matches and one is a mismatch, making this candidate a predominant Career Fit match.

Let me give you one more piece of insight here. You've heard the saying, "The only constant is change." Realize that jobs also constantly evolve and undergo change. Try to anticipate any upcoming changes or shifts in responsibilities or required skills, and incorporate these into your assessments of both interests and skills. A new hire with a 60 percent job match may only be a 40 percent job match six months down the road, and that will have a negative effect on motivation. I always recommend an estimated 70 percent to 80 percent match between the candidate and the job whenever possible. A strong predominant match will have a positive effect on motivation, and also allow room for change without significant negative impact.

Please note that although the preceding example looks like someone we would want to hire, it was only used to demonstrate the principles of assessment. It doesn't provide all of the information necessary to make a hiring decision.

Now that we have completed Part II, "Identifying High Performers" (the information-gathering portion of the interview process), it's time to talk about making the hiring decision.

Notes

1. Barbara Corcoran (@BarbaraCorcoran), Twitter, August 3, 2017, 6:10 a.m., https://twitter.com/BarbaraCorcoran/status/893096716907446273.

Part III

Hiring High Performers

Chapter 10
Hiring Words of Wisdom: To Hire or Not to Hire?

Many employers confuse hiring the most-skilled or qualified candidates as being equivalent to hiring high performers. It is not. Candidates with the right skills and experience can end up being high, average, or even poor performers. Neither skill nor qualifications determine performance level, thus exposing an enormous problem with the way many employers make hiring decisions. Ultimately, employers want to hire high performers—the people who are self-motivated, care about the quality of their work and produce the best results. In a nutshell, the goal is to hire skilled, self-motivated people who produce results.

Interviewer Impact

Without making the correlation between employee job performance and the employee selection process, there cannot be significant improvement in an organization's overall productivity. The false assumption that the selection process is working just fine and employee disengagement is related only to things that occur after the hire must be thrown out. Employers need a new awareness of the significant role that their interviewers and hiring process play in their organization's overall success. Certainly, great working environments with fewer barriers are wonderful, but it's not perfect conditions that create maximum performance; it's something inside of

> Employers neither make nor break
> high performers—they hire them!

each person that does. High performers don't achieve better results because the path to success was made easier. They achieve better results because they figure out a way when others don't. They rise above their conditions, challenges, and setbacks. Employers neither make nor break high performers—they hire them!

The MBI Hiring Standard

Let's talk hiring decisions. It's not enough for interviewers to learn the content of the previous nine chapters on understanding and identifying high performers. They must also adopt the MBI "hire *only* high performers" hiring standard. The days of making hiring decisions based on skill level alone or based on the interviewer's gut instinct are gone, obsolete, kaput. Just any hiring decision will no longer do.

So, what does adopting the MBI hiring standard look like? The answer is that for candidates to be considered high performers, they must demonstrate the following:

» At a minimum, satisfactory skill (this is a rating of three or higher for each required job skill)
» A predominant internal locus of control
» A predominant Career Fit match

This means we are hiring candidates who have adequately demonstrated that they are indeed high performers. It also means we are not hiring candidates who haven't. This is steadfast—with only one exception. If a candidate possesses both components of self-motivation—a predominant internal locus of control and a predominant Career Fit match—the option is to hire that person and provide training. Here's an added note: this only works if there are time and resources available to train. If someone must hit the ground running, such as a tax accountant hired in the middle of tax season, providing training and foregoing the skills would not be a viable option. However, sometimes organizations are too quick to write off this option. Perhaps there's no training program in place or maybe it's just never been done before. I've seen some very creative solutions when it comes to resolving this challenge. I encourage you to keep an open mind.

Candidates who lack the skills but have the other two high performer components technically aren't called "high performers." Instead, their title is "high potential." I like to think of them as future high performers. Considering candidates with inadequate skills is not an option if training is genuinely not possible. To recap, other than the exception for high potentials, the MBI hiring standard states that only high performers can be hired.

For some interviewers, this can take some getting used to. In the past, we made hiring decisions with skill being the only component considered, and either the candidate had it or didn't. Now we're talking about incorporating two more components, to make a total of three that must be considered when making our hiring decisions. That means candidates could have the perfect set of skills we need but not have the right attitude or be a mismatch for Career Fit, or both. Now what? Admit it—you love those skills! You even love the freedom to make hiring decisions based on whom you like and don't like. But just like Dorothy arriving in Oz, you're not in Kansas anymore. The specific purpose of the MBI hiring standard is to improve quality-of-hire. It helps us hire more high performers and avoid making some costly hiring mistakes—and that's a very good thing!

MBI Stats

People often share with me how much MBI has changed the way they hire and who they hire, for the better. Some tell me stories about the great employees they've hired using MBI that they would've turned away in the past. Others tell me how the locus of control assessment saved them from making a hiring mistake by exposing a candidate's lack of follow-through or pattern of excuses. You can now see the signs before extending an offer rather than after.

One Palm Beach County nonprofit with 350 employees had 48 percent annual turnover in their largest division before switching to MBI. Nearly half of their annual turnover resulted from employees who worked less than a year; this is known as short-term turnover. (Short-term turnover is an excellent indicator of hiring effectiveness.) This workplace was a metaphorical revolving door. People were hired and then turned around and quit or got terminated. It seemed as if their HR staff was doing almost nothing except recruiting. Upon closer examination, 85 percent of their short-term turnover also failed to meet job expectations. That's a large percentage. Let me explain this a little more. This organization wasn't having a mass exiting of high performers. For that to happen, first they would have had to hire high performers, and they hadn't. The vast majority of their new hires (85 percent) never performed well. So while on the surface this organization looked like it had a turnover problem, what it actually had was a *hiring* problem. The real wake-up call occurred when they put together their quality-of-hire metrics and saw the actual numbers. That's what ultimately motivated them to implement a plan to make changes to their hiring process.

This organization implemented MBI. They started by training all of their hiring managers. These managers ranged from having anywhere from one year to over twenty years of experience at making hiring decisions, with six years being the average. Nine of the thirteen interviewers had no formal training of any kind on how to interview or hire. An MBI workshop was conducted onsite to teach MBI to their hiring managers as well as their HR staff. Next, effective questions and MBI interview guides were developed and deployed. Hiring results continued to be tracked going forward.

> **Keep this in mind: you never want to focus on retention before improving your quality-of-hire.**

A noticeable improvement could be seen in the hiring results within the first ninety days. After more than a year's worth of data was collected, that 85 percent dropped to 10 percent and short-term turnover was reduced by more than 50 percent by using MBI. Even though there were still a few who didn't stay a full year, all of their new hires now met or exceeded job expectations (except for one). We're talking about a huge improvement in quality-of-hire. Now that the organization had effective hiring practices that were producing consistently good results, they were able to focus on retaining their good hires. If you want to learn more about this organization and how they gathered and tracked their metrics, it's available on the Hire Authority website.

Keep this in mind: you never want to focus on retention before improving your quality-of-hire.

The MBI Hiring Standard Meets the Interview Guide

The hiring standard is a very important part of MBI; so much so that it's been incorporated into the interview guide. On the last page of your interview guide, at the very bottom, these three yes-or-no questions should always be included. (They're already incorporated on every custom interview guide you generate on the Hire Authority membership site.) All three of the questions must be answered yes by the interviewer for a candidate to meet the MBI minimum hiring standards. Here are the questions:

1. Candidate demonstrated satisfactory skill— three or higher—or will train?   YES / NO
2. Candidate demonstrated a predominantly internal locus of control?   YES / NO
3. Candidate demonstrated a predominant Career Fit match?   YES / NO

MBI merely uses the fundamental principles of what enables high performers to achieve above-average results in order to establish a hiring standard. All high performers share three ingredients in common, therefore, the MBI hiring standard requires all three of these ingredients be present in a single person to consider hiring that person: 1 + 1 + 1 = high performer. When we start subtracting one or more of the high-performer ingredients, the total will no longer add up to a high performer. One plus one will never equal three, and the presence of one component alone will never add up to great performance.

Alright, so let's assume that you just finished interviewing someone and you're reviewing their scores. They earned threes, fours and fives for their answers to the skill portion of the O-SAE questions. The candidate gets a yes for demonstrating satisfactory skill, meaning they scored a three or higher for each skill. Skill scores are not added together and divided by the number of skills to get an average. It doesn't work that way. It's about the individual skill scores. Continuing, there were thirteen locus of control questions in total, eleven from the O-SAE questions plus the two woven into the Career Fit questions. Eight answers were scored internal and five of them external. Again, the answer is yes, the candidate demonstrated a predominantly internal locus of control. Two out of three (skill and the right attitude) are not enough; however, we need that third component. Out of the five Career Fit questions, the candidate scored four matches and one mismatch. We have our third yes: the candidate demonstrated a predominant Career Fit match.

This candidate meets the MBI hiring standard, but just because we have three yeses doesn't mean we have to hire this candidate. With a robust pool of applicants and a well-trained recruiting department, you may have more than one high performer to choose from. This is where you might choose the strongest skill set or "I can" attitude. Just make sure your decision is bias-free.

Consensus Decision

More often than not, there is more than one interviewer involved in making a hiring decision. The whole purpose of having multiple interviewers is to get the input of others. Hiring decisions should not be made by interviewers voting and saying yea or nay. You want to come to a consensus decision instead. Consensus decisions are a collective judgment. They are a way of reaching an agreement between all members of the interviewing team. Instead of simply voting and having the majority get their way, a group using consensus is committed to making a decision that everyone actively supports or at least can live with. I suggest you appoint a leader who can keep the discussion moving toward a decision. This might be a recruiter who has been involved from the start or an interviewer who will be the direct supervisor of the hired employee. One by one, interviewers should talk about their assessments and use their interview notes to defend their positions. The team should come to a consensus on whether the candidate meets the MBI hiring standard and should be offered a job or not.

During instructor-led MBI training, attendees watch a video interview and individually score a candidate's skill, locus of control, and Career Fit. Then they are broken into groups to make a consensus hiring decision. A spokesperson is selected to debrief and speak on behalf of their group. It's not uncommon for them to talk about how their interviewers scored answers differently. It may not be a big deal if one interviewer rated the candidate's skill a three and another rated that same answer a four. It can become a bigger deal in the locus of control and Career Fit scores, especially if it's enough to flip the predominant response in the other direction. I've even seen interviewers who get the scoring wrong go on to convince everyone in their group that their score is right. It gets interesting sometimes. We show a revisited version of the video where the candidate answers the same question but very differently. Those who score it incorrectly the first time around quickly realize their error. It's a great training exercise that allows people to learn from their mistakes before leaving the class. My point here is simple: don't allow yourself to be swayed too easily regarding your candidate assessments, because you just may be right.

Consensus decisions are beneficial because of the discussion they produce. Additional eyes and ears can also be valuable in catching and avoiding hiring mistakes. Be very cautious in regard to having a mixture of MBI-trained interviewers and untrained interviewers on your interviewing team, however. The untrained interviewer's input, especially when it's coming from someone in a higher-level position, can alter the teams hiring direction and not always for the better.

When it comes to making your hiring decision, let's address all the good reasons for compromising, or settling for less, should a candidate you really like fall short. Hmmm. Thinking... alright, we're done with that topic; let's move on to the next. Seriously, there is no good reason to hire an underperformer. However, hiring managers often try to make a bad reason sound legitimate by saying, "I didn't have a high performer in my pool of applicants." My reply is always, "Okay, so what are you doing to increase your pool of applicants?"

Regarding Recruiting

Technology may have changed how we receive job applications and résumés, but that didn't make some of the old ways obsolete. Many are still highly effective but forgotten. There are a few points I want to make regarding recruiting. First, let me give a shout-out to recruiters: I think your jobs are so much more important than what you get credit for! Just like the interviewers themselves, many organizations fail to recognize the valuable and time-saving role these prescreeners and first-round interviewers play. That being said, if you are going to use a recruiting firm, make sure you choose one whose staff has been trained on MBI.

One of the least expensive and most effective ways to increase the flow of applicants is to turn every employee into a recruiter. There are two ways to do this, and it's not an either-or—do both. First, let me mention recruiting cards. If you're not familiar with them, you can see what one looks like on the Hire Authority website. They are basically business cards that say, "I'm Impressed!" On the back, it has your contact information and states, "If you're ever looking to change jobs, please give me a call." You don't give these out to just anyone or everyone. When you come across someone who impresses you and could possibly fill a vacancy in your organization, that's when you hand out a card. I knew a grocery store manager who was always on the lookout for high performers. He visited a nearby sandwich shop regularly, and the woman behind the counter who often served him consistently gave customers noticeably superior service. He took note and gave her a recruiting card. He said that he always carried some with him. It didn't happen right away, but about two months later she showed up at the grocery store asking about employment opportunities. She was interviewed and hired on the spot. When you come across great hires, don't let them get away. The new trend is for hiring managers to be proactively involved in recruiting to fill their own positions.

Next, when it comes to recruiting, realize that your employees know people and they have friends, family, and neighbors who know people too. One of them may know someone who is job hunting or would consider a job change for the right opportunity. I can't even imagine how many missed opportunities are happening all the time. So, my question to you is, Does your organization have an effective in-house referral program? Does it a pay a referral bonus?

How much does it pay? If no one knows about it or if the bonus isn't lucrative enough, then your program may as well not exist. One organization had a two-phased payment program that paid $150 after a referred hire completed twelve weeks of management training and then another $100 on the anniversary date of that manager, a whooping $250 that took a year to earn. Do I need to mention they got very few referrals? I'm not sure whether that's because no one knew about it or because no one cared about it. This is an example of an ineffective program.

In-house referral programs can increase your pool of applicants, but first you must make the reward enticing. It doesn't even have to be a monetary reward; it could be an Apple Watch or another creative idea that would interest your employees. I recommend organizations know their cost-per-hire and make the value of a referral bonus somewhere just below that amount. Next, you must communicate the program every creative way you can and keep communicating it. This isn't a onetime announcement. Perhaps even more important is the confetti and balloons. When someone refers a successful hire and receives the bounty, make a big deal of it! Take a photo. Post it everywhere it's appropriate. That's what gets people excited and motivated. If you don't have the time to do it yourself, delegate it to someone who loves doing this type of thing.

Employees don't typically refer people who are unreliable or known to do a poor job. It could be because they wouldn't want to work with that person or they are afraid of a bad referral damaging their own reputation. But let's say they don't care about any of those and only want the referral bonus. All they see are the dollar signs. Don't be so afraid of this happening that you stay silent about your referral program. Don't be fearful of paying a bonus for a bad hire. All you have to do is explain in advance that all referrals are appreciated but must go through the hiring process just like any other job candidate. Then, as the interviewer, take no shortcuts. Conduct a full MBI interview and only hire the high performers. There's nothing that says you must hire every referral. I've hired some great ones and passed on a lot more. My point here is that an in-house referral program can be a great way to expand your pool of applicants, in addition to your existing recruiting methods. The cost is lower than the average cost-per-hire, and it's easy. What's not to like?

> **Don't turn a recruiting problem into a hiring problem or even a management nightmare by having to clean up the mess your bad hires create.**

When you don't have a high performer among the candidates you have interviewed, you always have the option to keep looking. I understand it can be difficult to find and hire someone when few people are applying and you have no one else to interview. It's just another challenge, and one that requires a creative recruiting solution. *Bad hires are never the solution.* Don't turn a recruiting problem into a hiring problem or even a management nightmare by having to clean up the mess your bad hires create.

Respect the Process!

We must always respect the MBI process and take no shortcuts! To do that, it takes interviewers who have been properly trained in MBI (that means every interviewer involved), who ask effective interview questions, and who follow the MBI hiring standard. All three are required to achieve maximum hiring results. Too often I hear people confess to taking shortcuts to the MBI training. Resist the temptation of giving a fellow interviewer a summarized course, thinking it will be enough for them to get by. One time I was speaking at a conference in Nashville. A woman came up to me and said she had been using MBI for about a year and liked it. I asked her how she learned it; I was wondering if she read the book, took the online course, or was taught by an instructor. She said that she heard me speak about it the year before.

Let me be clear, when I talk about MBI at conferences, which I do a lot, I explain the basics about what it is and how it works. I'm not actually teaching it. An instructor-led class takes a full day, that is, eight hours. When I speak at a conference, it's usually for about sixty minutes. Even if I tried to cram it into four hours, I'd have to leave out half of the content. It would be like reading every other chapter in this book! Just imagine how much gets left out. There was, of course, no way this woman actually learned MBI well enough to use it effectively, or really at all. But it gets worse, even bordering on ridiculous. Sometimes people tell me they've taught MBI to everyone in their department by giving them a twenty-minute crash course. There's no way in twenty minutes, or in three hours, someone can learn everything they need to know to use MBI: the process of achievement, where it breaks down, the power of attitude, the role passion plays in performance, how these two come together to create the highest level of self-motivation, how to write effective O-SAE questions, the three rules that must always be followed, not to mention the five Career Fit questions and how they work, how to assess and score, and so on. Get my point? Those who get a "crash course" on MBI are getting shortchanged. There's no such thing as a crash course in MBI.

This isn't what bothers me the most, however—it's people who think they are using MBI, but really aren't. They're making hiring mistakes that they otherwise wouldn't, and when they do, they're going to think MBI doesn't work when it really does. *There are no shortcuts.* Resist the urge of giving anyone a crash course and buy a copy of this book for every interviewer you know instead. They'll thank you—trust me! I have been using and teaching MBI for more than twenty years. I know what it takes for people to produce the best hiring results with it—so please do me a favor and don't dilute it. That serves no one's best interest.

I see the best hiring results when the directive to improve quality-of-hire comes from the top down, at the CEO or COO level, so that the entire organization is committed to hiring the best. When interviewers are held accountable for their hiring decisions, it has a magical way of improving hiring results. Some interviewers insist on doing their own thing no matter what. There needs to be someone with sufficient authority who can reel them in. Sometimes that person needs to be an executive.

> *There are no shortcuts.*

My success, and the success of many others using MBI, has been great. However, results are dependent upon a number of factors such as the skill of the interviewer, their openness to learning, how often they interview, how well they implement their MBI training, and their attitude, to mention a few. Because these factors vary from one individual to another, there is no guarantee of specific hiring results using MBI. No promise is being made or implied that you, or anyone else using MBI, will only hire high performers or will never have a bad hire. The bottom line is each interviewer is solely responsible for their own hiring decisions.

More Words of Hiring Wisdom

Now that I told you not to shortchange the process, I want you to go faster. *Faster!* Because of the pain of past hiring mistakes and a strong desire to avoid future ones, some organizations have needlessly padded their hiring process with time-consuming steps, including lots and lots of interviewers. One Atlanta-based company required the consensus of five directors before anyone could be hired. Sometimes that stretched out the time it took to make a hiring decision. Five high-level people couldn't all possibly miss a bad hire, right? Wrong. Another company in Texas required the input of so many interviewers it drove their recruiter nuts. First, they had to get all the interviewers to commit to a time and date that would work for everyone to interview each candidate. Then they had to get feedback from everyone. When and if they finally got a yes from everyone, many candidates had already moved on and accepted offers elsewhere. As a result of all the bureaucracy, they had to start the recruiting process all over again—only to have the same thing occur with the next candidate. A glut of interviews, especially involving interviewers who haven't been MBI trained, can stretch out a hiring process for far too long. Its intended effect—to screen out poor performers—typically backfires. Employers need to move their hiring process along faster, especially in a tight labor market when there are only a few applicants applying. I often ask candidates that I'm interested in, "Where else are you interviewing and how far along are you in the process?" I will speed up a process just to make sure I get someone I've identified as a high performer rather than let them slip away. When it comes to hiring high performers, I play to win—and so should you!

> When it comes to hiring high performers,
> I play to win—and so should you!

So how much time should you spend interviewing a candidate? I'm often asked this question. My answer is that it varies: it varies depending on the job, the candidate, and the interviewer. I am a very effective interviewer. I know exactly what information I want and how to get it. I maintain control over the interview and the information-gathering process. I can get what I need in one hour or less. Sometimes, if I get enough information to clearly knock a candidate from consideration, I will end the interview early. The real answer to the question, however, is that it takes as long as required for you, the interviewer, to know what you want to do next with the candidate. Do you want to continue moving that person forward in your hiring process or not? You cannot end the interview not knowing. You can't say, "I don't know if I'm interested in the candidate or not." You can't leave it in limbo. It's better to spend some extra time interviewing now rather than having to bring the candidate back for a second interview with you. In case you don't realize, MBI can be used to fill any and every job opening from entry level to CEO, and in any size organization from a start-up to *Fortune* 500 company. In fact, no job should be filled *without* using MBI.

Free MBI Resources

As we near the end of this book, I want to provide some great MBI resources that are available to you at no cost. My words of wisdom to you are to use them! They will help you to move forward as you implement MBI for yourself and for your entire organization. These resources include tutorials, a newsletter worth subscribing to, a LinkedIn group that can offer support, and even a fun quiz to test your hiring IQ. All of them, or links to them, are available on the Hire Authority website under the "Free MBI Resources" tab. Let me start with the newsletter. It's called *The Hire Awakening*. It offers success tips, great articles and related news. You can subscribe at www.hireauthority.com/subscribe. Since there is so much information out there for job seekers, it's nice to have a place to go that's dedicated to the hiring side of the interview. The Motivation-Based Interviewing LinkedIn group is that place. There you can find like-minded people, including some Certified MBI Trainers, who are passionate about hiring high performers.

Make sure you join the group, and while you're at it, make a point to connect with me on LinkedIn too.

On to the tutorials. Presently there are three. You already know about the one on how to track your quality-of-hire. It has the downloadable ready-to-use, six-tab Excel spreadsheet plus instructions. Make sure you check that one out. There is also the "Interviewer Law School" tutorial. It's about avoiding litigation. However, it tackles the topic from a unique perspective: why job seekers file discrimination claims. It provides information and advice beneficial to all interviewers. It also includes a ten-question test. Your job is to determine whether an interview question is okay to ask or not. The last tutorial is a highly interactive one on writing effective MBI questions. It won't teach you how to write MBI questions, but it's is a great refresher. It requires that you select only effective MBI questions and gives you detailed feedback as you go. Also, if you are active on Twitter you can find me at @CQAttitude.

All of these resources were created for you, the MBI interviewer, for the purpose of setting you and your organization up for the best possible hiring results. I am dedicated to that cause.

Certified Interviewers, CI

Effective interviewing begins with the right training and ends with a certification. Everyone involved in the employee selection process should become a *Certified Interviewer* before being allowed to participate in hiring new employees (see Figure 10.1). What exactly is a "Certified Interviewer"? It's someone who has successfully demonstrated the knowledge required to be an effective interviewer for the purpose of maximizing quality-of-hire. Since hiring impacts every aspect of an organization, it's one of the most important tasks that managers (and recruiters) do. Certification is a commitment to hiring excellence.

Figure 10.1. Certified Interviewer, CI

One organization struggling with quality-of-hire issues and high turnover required everyone involved in the employee selection process to not only learn MBI, but also become Certified Interviewers. Furthermore, anyone who didn't could not interview or make hiring decisions going forward. That would be a problem for their recruiters, managers, and even district managers. There would be no way they could do their job and fill job vacancies without conducting interviews. The top echelon was serious. They were committed to the organization being great, and it couldn't be great without hiring being done well. All interviewers were being held accountable for learning MBI, for using it properly, and perhaps most importantly, they were being held accountable for their hiring decisions via quality-of-hire and turnover metrics.

Part of becoming a Certified Interviewer requires taking an online exam. The exam is based on current best practices to achieve maximum hiring results, which means it's based on motivation-based interviewing and not behavior-based interviewing. The exam includes topics outside of MBI that are also important for interviewers to have knowledge of. Some of these additional topics include how to avoid litigation, quality-of-hire basics, and the impact that the interviewer's hiring decisions have on the organization as a whole. Exam questions for these non-MBI topics are generated from white papers that are available to read free of charge in the Exam Resource & Prep Center on the certification website.

Passing the exam means the interviewer can use the credentials *CI* after their name. For more information on becoming certified, visit www.Certified-Interviewer.com (don't forget the hyphen).

The Big MBI Bonus

By now you've likely come to realize that MBI training isn't just your average interviewer training of the past. But did you realize that it doesn't just teach how to hire? The benefits of providing MBI training within any organization go well beyond just improving quality-of-hire. What MBI training teaches about the process of achievement, the power of attitude, and what makes high achievers different is invaluable. Consider this: If you were to give someone a lecture about their attitude in hopes of improving their performance, they'd likely tune you out. The message could be just what they need to hear but they're not interested. When the same information is delivered via MBI training, however, it becomes safe to listen to. That's because we're talking about someone else's attitude: the job candidate's. Nonetheless, the information still gets in and gets processed. That's a breakthrough alone! From there, it can't help but be internalized. Privately, attendees would ask themselves, "How effective is my own attitude? Does it have room for improvement? Could I achieve better results by being more optimistic and less negative?" This typically happens quietly, but have no doubt, it's happening. I've seen it time and time again: the light bulb coming on in people's heads. It can be life changing! If that isn't good enough, it gets better.

What comes next can be summed up in two words: peer pressure. Do you know how many times on lunch breaks during MBI training coworkers and peers will catch someone in their group making an excuse and call them out on it? The person who was late to class will start talking about why and explain how the traffic was so bad. What happens next is priceless. One of their peers will say, "That's an external comment. You could have left your house earlier." Do you comprehend what just happened and how powerful it is? The potent message that's woven into MBI—that every human being has the power to achieve great results and it all starts with a person's attitude—catches on and permeates the organizational culture. People call out the ineffective behaviors of their coworkers. Behavior that was once tolerated becomes socially, or organizationally, unacceptable and the culture begins to shift. As new jobs open, MBI is used to fill them with optimists who are passionate about solving problems and don't make excuses when they fall short. They seek to improve themselves instead. For those who are already employed, many become motivated to shift their own attitude to one that's more conducive to success.

> **Truly, the single greatest loss of human potential is the "I can't" attitude.**

Truly, the single greatest loss of human potential is the "I can't" attitude. The single greatest loss of organizational potential is the culture of mediocrity that is created when employers hire people with ineffective attitudes. This culture is further fueled by the flawed notion that human beings have the power to change other human beings. A quantum leap forward in productivity is at hand, but that cannot and will not occur until employers shift their perspective, not just in regard to how they hire and who they hire, but also by recognizing that employee engagement is not the way forward. It's difficult to say where MBI will have the most profound impact—the hiring results, the organizational culture, or the shift in attitude that MBI inspires. No matter the answer, it's a game changer!

Happy twentieth anniversary, MBI!

Bibliography

Abadi, Mark. "Eagles Quarterback Nick Foles' Super Bowl Victory Speech Has an Important Lesson about Failure." *Business Insider*, February 8, 2018. http://www.businessinsider.com/nick-foles-super-bowl-speech-failure-2018-2.

Clifton, Donald O., and Paula Nelson. "Let the Rabbits Run: A Parable," in *Soar with Your Strengths: A Simple Yet Revolutionary Philosophy of Business and Management*. New York: Dell Publishing, 1992: 3–8.

Collins, Jim. *Good to Great: Why Some Companies Make the Leap and Others Don't*. New York: HarperCollins, 2001.

Sinek, Simon. *Start with Why: How Great Leaders Inspire Everyone to Take Action*. New York: Portfolio/Penguin, 2009.

Index

About the Author

Carol Quinn is the creator of motivation-based interviewing (MBI), the fastest-growing interviewing method for identifying and hiring top-performing employees. Her thirty years of interviewing experience and her passion for hiring high performers led to the creation of Hire Authority, an organization dedicated to teaching thousands how to hire the best using MBI.

Carol's cutting-edge employee selection methodology is now taught and used globally, and she's become a popular keynote speaker on the power of attitude, an important ingredient all high performers share. Along with her nomination for a prestigious Innovation in Delivering Breakthrough Solutions award by a *Fortune* 500 client, she's been endorsed by Walt Disney Executive Vice President Lee Cockerell (now retired). Lee dedicated an entire chapter in his book *The Customer Rules: The 39 Essential Rules for Delivering Sensational Service* to Carol and MBI. Renowned management expert Ken Blanchard, bestselling coauthor of *The One Minute Manager*, also endorsed Carol's first edition MBI book, *Don't Hire Anyone without Me!*

Carol Quinn is the author of four books to date, and she is passionate about teaching others how the hidden power of attitude within all of us can make amazing things happen. Carol's most requested keynote speech, "Experience the Attitude," is a powerful and compelling presentation designed to help awaken and unleash the power of achievement from within.

If you would like Carol to speak at an upcoming corporate event, convention, or conference on this topic, on MBI, or on any of her other topics of expertise, please send Carol an email at Speaker@ CarolQuinn.com.

Become a Certified MBI Trainer

What Are Certified MBI Trainers?

Certified MBI Trainers are individuals who have successfully completed the Hire Authority MBI Train-the-Trainer class. They have demonstrated an advanced understanding of MBI along with a proficiency in presenting the official MBI training materials. Certified Trainers receive a comprehensive facilitator guide, the MBI PowerPoint presentation, and MBI training videos. MBI is a licensed training program. These are two types of Certified Trainers.

Corporate MBI Trainers

Corporate trainers work within their organization to teach MBI to everyone involved in their employee selection process. It's a cost-effective way to deliver MBI training in-house as needed.

Contract MBI Trainers

Contract trainers are skilled independent business, management, training, or HR consultants who conduct MBI workshops for their clients as well as for Hire Authority's clients.

For additional information on becoming a Certified MBI Trainer, including class dates, please visit our website at: www.Hire Authority.com.

Contact us directly at: 561-231-0313
Or email us at: info@hireauthority.com

About Hire Authority

Additional Ways To Learn MBI

Online Web Course—This comprehensive, self-paced, interactive course is the fastest way to learn MBI. It's an excellent option for any size business or for independent professionals.

Onsite Training—MBI instructor-led classroom training conducted at your corporate location(s) offers an added degree of interactivity and group participation that can greatly enhance the learning experience.

Workshops Open To The Public—We offer instructor-led workshops that anyone can attend. Held at various locations, these workshops are a great way for small groups or individuals to learn MBI.

Additional MBI Products & Services

MBI Interview Guide Generator Membership—Create your MBI Interview Guides in minutes. Just click, drag, and print. We've got a database that includes 750+ effective MBI interview questions to chose from.

MBI Affiliate Referral Program—Earn revenue referring the MBI web course training. We provide you with marketing banners and a unique link to share. Whenever someone you referred purchases the MBI web course training, we'll pay you a generous percentage of the sale. There's no cost to you... and your clients will thank you!

For additional information please visit www.HireAuthority.com.
Contact us directly at: 561-231-0313
Or email us at: info@hireauthority.com

Other SHRM Titles

A Manager's Guide to Developing Competencies in HR Staff
Tips and Tools for Improving Proficiency in Your Reports
Phyllis G. Hartman, SHRM-SCP

California Employment Law: A Guide for Employers
Revised and Updated 2018 Edition
James J. McDonald, Jr., JD

Digital HR
A Guide to Technology-Enabled HR
Deborah Waddill, Ed.D.

From Hello to Goodbye: Second Edition
Proactive Tips for Maintaining Positive Employee Relations
Christine V. Walters, JD, SHRM-SCP

From We Will to At Will
A Handbook for Veteran Hiring, Transitioning, and Thriving in the Workplace
Justin Constantine with Andrew Morton

Go Beyond the Job Description
A 100-Day Action Plan for Optimizing Talents and Building Engagement
Ashley Prisant Lesko, Ph.D., SHRM-SCP

The HR Career Guide
Great Answers to Tough Career Questions
Martin Yate, CPC

HR on Purpose!!
Developing Deliberate People Passion
Steve Browne, SHRM-SCP

Mastering Consultation as an HR Practitioner
Making an Impact on Small Businesses
Jennifer Currence, SHRM-SCP

Motivation-Based Interviewing
A Revolutionary Approach to Hiring the Best
Carol Quinn

The Practical Guide to HR Analytics
Using Data to Inform, Transform, and Empower HR Decisions
Shonna D. Waters, Valerie N. Streets, Lindsay A. McFarlane, and Rachel Johnson-Murray

The Power of Stay Interviews for Engagement and Retention
Second Edition
Richard P. Finnegan

Predicting Business Success
Using Smarter Analytics to Drive Results
Scott Mondore, Hannah Spell, Matt Betts, and Shane Douthitt

The Recruiter's Handbook
A Complete Guide for Sourcing, Selecting, and Engaging the Best Talent
Sharlyn Lauby, SHRM-SCP

The SHRM Essential Guide to Employment Law
A Handbook for HR Professionals, Managers, and Businesses
Charles H. Fleischer, JD

The Talent Fix
A Leader's Guide to Recruiting Great Talent
Tim Sackett, SHRM-SCP

Books Approved for SHRM Recertification Credits

107 Frequently Asked Questions About Staffing Management, Fiester (ISBN: 9781586443733)

47 Frequently Asked Questions About the Family and Medical Leave Act, Fiester (ISBN: 9781586443801)

57 Frequently Asked Questions About Workplace Safety and Security, Fiester (ISBN: 9781586443610)

97 Frequently Asked Questions About Compensation, Fiester (ISBN: 9781586443566)

A Manager's Guide to Developing Competencies in HR Staff, Hartman (ISBN: 9781586444365)

A Necessary Evil: Managing Employee Activity on Facebook, Wright (ISBN: 9781586443412)

Aligning Human Resources and Business Strategy, Holbeche (ISBN: 9780750680172)

Applying Advanced Analytics to HR Management Decisions, Sesil (ISBN: 9780133064605)

Applying Critical Evaluation: Making an Impact in Small Business, Currence (ISBN: 9781586444426)

Becoming the Evidence Based Manager, Latham (ISBN: 9780891063988)

Being Global: How to Think, Act, and Lead in a Transformed World, Cabrera (ISBN: 9781422183229)

Black Holes and White Spaces: Reimagining the Future of Work and HR, Boudreau (ISBN: 9781586444617)

Business Literacy Survival Guide for HR Professionals, Garey (ISBN: 9781586442057)

Business-Focused HR: 11 Processes to Drive Results, Mondore (ISBN: 9781586442040)

Calculating Success, Hoffman (ISBN: 9781422166390)

California Employment Law, Revised and Updated, McDonald (ISBN: 9781586444815)

Collaborate: The Art of We, Sanker (ISBN: 9781118114728)

Deep Dive: Proven Method for Building Strategy, Horwath (ISBN: 9781929774821)

Defining HR Success: 9 Critical Competencies for HR Professionals, Alonso (ISBN: 9781586443825)

Destination Innovation: HR's Role in Charting the Course, Buhler (ISBN: 9781586443832)

Developing Business Acumen, Currence (ISBN: 9781586444143)

Developing Proficiency in HR: 7 Self-Directed Activities for HR Professionals, Cohen (ISBN: 9781586444167)

Digital HR: A Guide to Technology-Enabled Human Resources, Waddill (ISBN: 9781586445423)

Diverse Teams at Work:
Capitalizing on the Power
of Diversity, Gardenswartz
(ISBN: 9781586440367)
Effective Human Resource Management:
A Global Analysis, Lawler
(ISBN: 9780804776875)
Emotional Intelligence 2.0, Bradberry
(ISBN: 9780974320625)
Financial Analysis for HR
Managers, Director
(ISBN: 9780133925425)
From Hello to Goodbye, 2e, Walters
(ISBN: 9781586444471)
From We Will to at Will: A Handbook
for Veteran Hiring, Constantine
(ISBN: 9781586445072)
Give Your Company a Fighting
Chance, Danaher
(ISBN: 9781586443658)
Go Beyond the Job Description, Lesko
(ISBN: 9781586445171)
Got a Minute? The 9 Lessons Every
HR Professional Must Learn
to Be Successful, Dwyer
(ISBN: 9781586441982)
Got a Solution? HR Approaches to
5 Common and Persistent
Business Problems, Dwyer
(ISBN: 9781586443665)
Handbook for Strategic HR: Best
Practices in Organization
Development, Vogelsang
(ISBN: 9780814432495)
Hidden Drivers of Success: Leveraging
Employee Insights for Strategic
Advantage, Schiemann
(ISBN: 9781586443337)
HR at Your Service: Lessons from
Benchmark Service Organizations,
Latham (ISBN: 9781586442477)
HR on Purpose: Developing Deliberate
People Passion, Browne
(ISBN: 9781586444259)

HR Transformation: Building Human
Resources from the Inside Out,
Ulrich (ISBN: 9780071638708)
HR's Greatest Challenge: Driving the
C-Suite to Improve Employee
Engagement ..., Finnegan
(ISBN: 9781586443795)
Investing in People: Financial
Impact of Human Resource
Initiatives, 2e, Boudreau
(ISBN: 9780132394116)
Investing in What Matters:
Linking Employees to
Business Outcomes, Mondore
(ISBN: 9781586441371)
Leading an HR Transformation,
Anderson
(ISBN: 9781586444860)
Lean HR: Introducing Process
Excellence to Your Practice, Lay
(ISBN: 9781481914208)
Linkage Inc.'s Best Practices for
Succession Planning: Case Studies,
Research, Models, Tools, Sobol
(ISBN: 9780787985790)
Looking to Hire an HR Leader, Hartman
(ISBN: 9781586443672)
Manager 3.0: A Millennial's Guide
to Rewriting the Rules
of Management, Karsh
(ISBN: 9780814432891)
Manager Onboarding: 5 Steps for Setting
New Leaders Up for Success, Lauby
(ISBN: 9781586444075)
Manager's Guide to Employee
Engagement, Carbonara
(ISBN: 9780071799508)
Managing Employee Turnover, Allen
(ISBN: 9781606493403)
Managing the Global
Workforce, Caligiuri
(ISBN: 9781405107327)

Managing the Mobile Workforce:
Leading, Building,
and Sustaining Virtual
Teams, Clemons
(ISBN: 9780071742207)
Managing the Older Worker:
How to Prepare for the New
Organizational Order, Cappelli
(ISBN: 9781422131657)
Mastering Consultation as an
HR Practitioner, Currence
(ISBN: 9781586445027)
Measuring ROI in Employee Relations
and Compliance, Phillips
(ISBN: 9781586443597)
Motivation-Based Interviewing:
A Revolutionary Approach
to Hiring the Best, Quinn
(ISBN: 9781586445478)
Multipliers: How the Best Leaders Make
Everyone Smarter, Wiseman
(ISBN: 9780061964398)
Negotiation at Work: Maximize Your
Team's Skills with 60 High-
Impact Activities, Asherman
(ISBN: 9780814431900)
Nine Minutes on Monday: The Quick
and Easy Way to Go from
Manager to Leader, Robbins
(ISBN: 9780071801980)
One Strategy: Organizing, Planning
and Decision Making, Sinofsky
(ISBN: 9780470560457)
People Analytics: How Social
Sensing Technology Will
Transform Business, Waber
(ISBN: 9780133158311)
Perils and Pitfalls of California
Employment Law: A Guide
for HR Professionals, Effland
(ISBN: 9781586443634)
Point Counterpoint II: New Perspectives
on People & Strategy, Vosburgh
(ISBN: 9781586444181)

Point Counterpoint: New Perspectives
on People & Strategy, Tavis
(ISBN: 9781586442767)
Practices for Engaging the 21st-Century
Workforce, Castellano
(ISBN: 9780133086379)
Predicting Business Success: Using
Smarter Analytics to
Drive Results, Mondore
(ISBN: 9781586445379)
Proving the Value of HR: How and
Why to Measure ROI, Phillips
(ISBN: 9781586442316)
Reality Based Leadership, Wakeman
(ISBN: 9780470613504)
Rethinking Retention in Good
Times and Bad, Finnegan
(ISBN: 9780891062387)
Social Media Strategies for Professionals
and Their Firms, Golden
(ISBN: 9780470633106)
Solving the Compensation Puzzle:
Putting Together a Complete Pay
and Performance System, Koss
(ISBN: 9781586440923)
Stop Bullying at Work, 2e, Daniel
(ISBN: 9781586443856)
Talent, Transformation, and the
Triple Bottom Line, Savitz
(ISBN: 9781118140970)
The ACE Advantage: How Smart
Companies Unleash Talent for
Optimal Performance, Schiemann
(ISBN: 9781586442866)
The Big Book of HR, Mitchell
(ISBN: 9781601631893)
The Crowdsourced Performance Review,
Mosley (ISBN: 9780071817981)
The Cultural Fit Factor: Creating
an Employment Brand
That Attracts ..., Pellet
(ISBN: 9781586441265)
The Definitive Guide to HR
Communication, Davis
(ISBN: 9780137061433)

The E-HR Advantage: The Complete Handbook for Technology-Enabled Human Resources, Waddill (ISBN: 9781904838340)

The Employee Engagement Mindset, Clark (ISBN: 9780071788298)

The EQ Interview: Finding Employees with High Emotional Intelligence, Lynn (ISBN: 9780814409411)

The Global Challenge: International Human Resource Management, Evans (ISBN: 9780073530376)

The Global M&A Tango, Trompenaars (ISBN: 9780071761154)

The HR Answer Book, 2e, Smith (ISBN: 9780814417171)

The HR Career Guide: Great Answers to Tough Career Questions, Yate (ISBN: 9781586444761)

The Manager's Guide to HR, 2e, Muller (ISBN: 9780814433027)

The Performance Appraisal Tool Kit, Falcone (ISBN: 9780814432631)

The Power of Appreciative Inquiry: A Practical Guide to Positive Change, Whitney (ISBN: 9781605093284)

The Power of Stay Interviews for Retention and Engagement, 2e, Finnegan (ISBN: 9781586445126)

The Practical Guide to HR Analytics, Waters (ISBN: 9781586445324)

The Recruiter's Handbook, Lauby (ISBN: 9781586444655)

The SHRM Essential Guide to Employment Law, Fleischer (ISBN: 9781586444709)

The Talent Fix: A Leader's Guide to Recruiting Great Talent, Sackett (ISBN: 9781586445225)

Touching People's Lives: Leaders' Sorrow or Joy, Losey (ISBN: 9781586444310)

Transformative HR: How Great Companies Use Evidence-Based Change ..., Boudreau (ISBN: 9781118036044)

Transformational Diversity, Citkin (ISBN: 9781586442309)

Up, Down, and Sideways: High-Impact Verbal Communication for HR Professionals, Buhler (ISBN: 9781586443375)

View from the Top: Leveraging Human and Organization Capital to Create Value, Wright (ISBN: 9781586444006)

What If? Short Stories to Spark Diversity Dialogue, Robbins (ISBN: 9780891062752)

What Is Global Leadership? 10 Key Behaviors that Define Great Global Leaders, Gundling (ISBN: 9781904838234)

Winning the War for Talent in Emerging Markets: Why Women are the Solution, Hewlett (ISBN: 9781422160602)